Vital Signs
of a
Healthy Church

A Diagnostic

Guy Chevreau

New Wine Press

New Wine Ministries
PO Box 17
Chichester
West Sussex
United Kingdom
PO19 2AW

ISBN 978-1-905991-01-3

Typeset by CRB Associates, Reepham, Norfolk
Cover design by CCD, www.ccdgroup.co.uk
Printed in Malta

"He can no longer have God for his Father,
who has not the Church for his mother."
(Cyprian, *On the Unity of the Church*, AD 251)[1]

"You are safe, who have God for your Father
and his Church for your mother."
(Augustine, AD 400)[2]

[1] *The Treatises of Cyprian*, I.6, *Ante-Nicene Fathers*, vol. 5, Hendrickson Pub., Peabody, Mass., 1994, p. 423.
[2] "In Answer to the Letters of Petilian, the Donatist," ch. 9, *Nicene and Post-Nicene Fathers*, First Series, vol. 4, Hendrickson Pub., Peabody, Mass., 1994, p. 601.

Vital Signs is dedicated to
Peter and Chris Drown and
Tom and Karen Henner.
Your encouragement, friendship and support
have kept body and soul together.
Bless your big hearts.

Contents

Acknowledgements

My heartfelt thanks go out to the several hundred pastors and churches that have hosted me these thirteen years. You have all enriched my life.

Thanks also to Lois Frances, Anne Fountain, Mike Bradley, Nev Green, Peter and Chris Drown, and Tom and Karen Henner. Our discussions about what should and shouldn't go into the book, and your careful reading of the manuscript, have made *Vital Signs* a much better book.

Thanks too to Tim Pettingale. That all authors should have such a gracious and accommodating publisher!

To my wife Janis: again, as first reader your critique is invaluable.

Guy Chevreau,
Oakville, Canada,
August 2007
S.D.G.

Foreword

As a church pastor I have found that one of the most common questions I am asked when meeting friends that I have not seen for a while is, "How is your church doing?" After about a year and a half into the role of senior pastor at The Gathering Place, I realized that it might be a good idea to actually have some idea of how to answer that question with both honesty and reality, rather than just giving the default answer of, "It's well, thanks; at least everyone hasn't left yet!"

I began to bring this question before the Lord in my times of prayer. I understood that it was important that I was able to truthfully answer the question of "how the church was doing" in the light of the priorities of the Spirit, rather than those of men. Obviously the answer lies in deeper things than just numbers of people attending or rebelling! I also understood that it was my responsibility as pastor to frequently ask this question in my times of prayer for the church and to listen very carefully to what the Lord had to say on the subject.

At just about the time that this question was at the forefront of my devotions, I received an email from Guy containing the draft of a sermon titled "Diagnostics." As I read through these notes I heard the Spirit say to me, "Here are the answers to the questions you've been asking of Me." My response to the email was, first, to ask what Guy was thinking in attempting to cover this whole subject in one sermon! Second, I asked Guy to put the material together for a weekend conference in which the church could undergo a spiritual check-up; a time in which we could all ask, "How are we doing?"

It is not just pastors who have the responsibility to ask this searching question. We all have a responsibility to constantly and consistently seek the Holy Spirit's conviction and correction, as well as receiving His encouragement and affirmation. The question is not only relevant to the church but also to the individual. This is a book not just for church pastors and leaders, but for any true disciple of Jesus Christ.

I have known Guy for about seven years. We have traveled together many times. We have shared many plane and car journeys, many disasters on the golf course and even shared one bed, though I choose not to dwell on that last memory! We have become very close friends, committed and submitted to each other.

Early in our relationship, after our second ministry trip together, I had an extremely vivid dream in which, while I had been asleep, Guy had entered my house and completely rearranged my kitchen! In my dream, I walked into my "new" kitchen to find Guy looking very pleased with himself. He had renewed and revitalized my old kitchen such that it was still the same room but looked and felt so much bigger and it had so much more in it. Guy then took me outside to my back garden. Once again he had managed to rearrange everything so that the garden was bigger, more beautiful, and with many more features and plants. Unlike the kitchen, the garden was unrecognizable as my own tiny plot.

I don't have that kind of dream all that often. When I do, I know that God is telling me something. Seven years on, I can truly say that Dr. Chevreau has completely renewed and revitalized my faith and my understanding of the truths of grace. He has opened up the Word of God and the world of God to me in ways that I would have never imagined. I am so thankful to God for this gift of such a great friend and my own personal Bible School lecturer!

It may be that you are reading this book with little or no knowledge of the author. It is an over-used word today, but Guy has a truly *Apostolic* ministry to the Church. His ministry mandate, "to serve, to bless, to build," is a succinct role-description for the apostle. It only serves and blesses the Church to build on firm and well-built foundations and footings. To my mind, this is the most representative book that Guy has written regarding his ministry to the Church. His role in the Church is similar to that of a doctor overseeing the health of his patients.

In considering the influence that Guy has had at The Gathering Place, it is difficult to differentiate that which has come direct from his visits to us and that which exists through his mentoring of me. What is clear is that the congregation respects and honors the authority and gifting that Guy has to speak into the life of the church, correcting and defining our theology as well as our practice. Our church feels "safe and secure" with Guy's teaching and both recognizes and values the importance of his input into its pastor and leadership. We have determined to host Guy regularly, at least one visit each year, to continue to receive further revelation through his teaching, but also to invite his diagnostic oversight.

Unlike the General Practitioner, who only has the expertise to check for the initial and vital signs of the patient, Dr. Guy Chevreau is also qualified to carry out the necessary intricate, exploratory and remedial surgery. I have "held the scalpel" and "mopped his brow" for him on many occasions and I have seen many a patient revived to life far beyond that which they were previously living.

Undoubtedly, the reading of this book will raise further issues. Each subject, considered in each chapter, is worthy of a book in its own right. Hopefully the reader will feel encouraged in some areas and challenged in others. The question that the reader must ask is, "What can I do about those symptoms that are showing cause for concern?" It may be that the patient needs to be referred. I have yet to meet anyone more qualified of the Holy Spirit than Guy Chevreau to whom those symptoms should be referred and I fully recommend that you do so.

Nev Green
Pastor of The Gathering Place Christian Fellowship
Blandford
England

Introduction

In 2005 I celebrated my fiftieth birthday. When my wife Janis asked what I wanted for a special present, I immediately responded, "A motorcycle!" I rode a Honda 500 in my late teens and early twenties, and I thought that it was high time to "let the good times roll" once again. Given my age, stage, and diet, my loving wife got me, instead, a colonoscopy. Unwisely, I declined the pre-process sedative.

When the results were in, I passed with flying colors, thus confirming my belief that as long as I eat beef that comes from a vegetarian cow then, between the two of us, we've got our greens covered.

Shortly after recovering from my birthday procedures, I was with a church that wasn't very healthy. Its vital signs were concerning and that got me thinking. Over the last thirteen years I've been privileged to work with over two hundred and thirty-five different churches worldwide. It has been an honor and a pleasure to be with some very healthy, happy, holy church families – churches that would and should be considered spiritually fit.

I have been with other churches, however, that are seriously overweight, some that have chronic heart problems, and a few that need to give up smoking. Several of them need to get some regular exercise, while others are desperately in need of some fiber in their diet. More than one is showing early signs of dementia.

As I continued these reflections a working thesis began to form in my mind and spirit: an unhealthy church is unlikely to see much by way of true spiritual growth. Little by way of either conversion or transformation ought to be expected. God loves the lost and hurting too much to entrust their care to a church that's sick, let alone one with contagious diseases.

Physiologically, medics assess four vital signs: temperature, pulse, blood pressure and respiration. These vital signs are considered the core basics of life. If the skin is cold to touch, there is no pulse and no sign of respiration, one doesn't have to worry about high blood pressure any longer.

My colonoscopy required prolonged preparation and the exam itself was, to say the least, invasive. Vital signs, in contrast, are very quickly and easily determined. They are near-immediate diagnoses, ones which are assessed within minutes. We don't have to wait on results like we do for other procedures like blood work or a CAT scan.

This book is proposed as a spiritual diagnostic that assesses the vital signs of a local church. I have preached my way through the material several times and have discussed these core basics at length with several friends. While the focus is predominantly on the corporate life of a local church, there are certainly personal applications that we would each do well to consider as individuals.

At the outset it serves to recognize that very few of us like going to see our doctors. Rarely do we look forward to our annual physical. It's not that those in the medical profession are not nice people. Rather, we have a lurking fear that they will find something wrong with us. At the very least, we half expect them to tell us we're not as healthy as we should or could be.

If we're not afraid of the report we receive from our doctors, we certainly rue the day of our visit to the dentist. I for one know that Dr. Saunders is going to ask, as he always does, "Are you flossing regularly?" With absolute sincerity, I answer, "I am." I floss religiously, the night before my appointment, every single time. I know he knows that, so I wonder why he asks the question. As he then proceeds to scrape, scratch and pry away, I nurse the nagging reservation that my sins have certainly beset me and that some sort of decay or disease will be discovered. Surely I will not be among those who escape with big toothy smiles, the proud owners of new toothbrushes and those handy little rolls of floss. No. Once he's done with me, the drool will soon be sliding uncontrollably from both corners of my benumbed mouth and my cheeks will feel like I've been the loser in a beer brawl punch-up.

If we can exercise a bit of objectivity we would concede that it is not a health practitioner's job to make us feel good about ourselves, it's to make us feel better. Few of us look forward to the doctor's report after an exam – but it does afford us the opportunity to make changes that can have long lasting consequences for our health and wellbeing.

My dentist, for instance, tells me every visit, "You don't have to floss all your teeth. You only have to floss the ones you want to keep." I know flossing will improve my dental hygiene. The question is, do I care enough to be bothered to make the requisite changes?

As I've worked on *Vital Signs*, I have tried to discern the spiritual equivalents of the four physiological vital signs – those easily assessed dynamics that clearly reveal the relative health and wellbeing of a local church fellowship. The four I propose are: worship, leadership priorities, church atmosphere and generosity. Consideration will be given to each of these in turn, after which one further indicator requires attention.

I first preached through the initial material at the request of my friend, Nev Green. He had recently taken over as senior pastor of The Gathering Place, in Blandford Forum, Dorset, and as he put it, wanted "some help knowing how he was doing." During the evening debrief with the church's leadership team after our weekend together someone asked, "If there was a fifth vital sign for church health, what would it be?" With only a moment's thought, I answered, "Evangelism and mission."

This fifth dynamic seems a most appropriate and necessary

inclusion, because after the four physiological vital signs are assessed, the next thing the doctor does is check the ability of our eyes to focus. He or she says, "Follow my finger," and then waves it about. Spiritually, the equivalent question would be, "Where is the church looking?" or "Who is in their field of vision?"

The concluding chapter is based on the premise that, short of disaster and crisis, change typically comes by subtle increments. Having considered the corporate aspects of a healthy church, attention is given to the dynamics of the transformation the Lord works in our personal and corporate lives.

Several of my hosts and a number of friends encouraged me to develop the sermon series that was originally called "Diagnostics" and turn it into the present book. Among them was one host who, the Sunday after I preached the series, told the congregation that he felt "Diagnostics" had given them a baseline ministry manifesto. He went on to say, "These are our values. This teaching series is a really good way of establishing who we are, if any of you were confused."

Before I began writing, I reviewed the numerous books I have on church health and was assured that the material that has become *Vital Signs* could make several unique contributions. Many of the other works offer step-by-step guidelines for growing the local church. Others major on the success stories of the mega-churches and offer strategies that emulate their models. The message is often explicit: "Do what we do and you will get the same results."

Some of the other books offer statistical and analytical assessments drawn from studies of what makes healthy churches healthy. There is great merit in learning from good teachers, but given that most of us learn our lessons the hard way, such an approach ignores the valuable insights that can be gleaned from the battle-scarred.

The process of writing *Vital Signs* has been a continuous challenge. Never before have I typed so much that has been subsequently deleted. As a diagnostic I have tried to exercise ruthless discipline to keep from exceeding the evaluative mandate of the work. At many points throughout the book a number of issues beg further treatment, but engaging those considerations would be the spiritual equivalent of conducting exploratory surgery during a routine physical examination.

But if, after placing a cold stethoscope on our bare chest, the doctor hears an erratic heartbeat, further tests would be prescribed. An exercise stress test, a Holter monitor and an electrocardiogram would all help with further diagnosis. Abnormal results, in turn, could initiate potentially life-saving treatments including surgery.

It would be most unwise, even irresponsible to ignore the physician's concerns. Hoping that "it will just get better" is not just naïve, it is a misguided belief that may prove to be fatal.

Therefore, the following stories, observations and studied reflections are in no way definitive, exhaustive or comprehensive. I do hope they serve to evoke consideration, prayer and discernment. There is no Evaluation Score Sheet at the end of the book and no tick boxes to check and tally. Rather, I trust that the Spirit of God will use this material to inspire, convict and correct. Just as there may come a time when we have to brace ourselves when the doctor says, "You're not going to like what I have to tell you," it would be most unwise, even irresponsible to ignore the Spirit's witness when we don't like what we're hearing Him say. As the apostle James warns, *"Be sure you act on the message, and do not merely listen and so deceive yourselves"* (James 1:22).

When I began traveling as an international itinerant thirteen years ago, I believe the Lord gave me the mandate "to serve, to bless, to build." It is in that spirit that *Vital Signs* is offered.

1

Worship

As a visiting preacher my first exposure to the corporate dynamics of a local church is typically in our worship together. Like taking a person's pulse, I usually begin to have a sense of things quite quickly, sometimes within a song or two, and usually within a set. But let it be stated early – this discernment has nothing to do with musical style. I have had glorious times worshiping with Trappist monks as we chanted the Psalms in French and intoned the liturgy in Gregorian chant. I've soaked myself with sweat dancing with my African brothers and sisters as we sang innumerable "Hallelujah, Hosannas." I've been with Pentecostals who were so wild they would have handled snakes if there were any handy.[1] Style is not the issue. There is but one assessment: are we worshiping the Father "in Spirit and in truth"?

That is how Jesus responded to the Samaritan woman's question about the "hows" of worship: *True worshipers will worship the Father in Spirit and truth. These are the worshipers the Father wants"* (John 4:23). The Lord shifted her rather defensive, theoretical and abstract questions about religious ritual to the heart of worship, and it was the woman's problem with this very issue, intimacy, that had her failed love life in such a mess.

What is true worship like? The Greek word used in this passage is *proskuneis* and it means to "throw oneself down." But true worship is no longer a question of the externals of place and posture, where and how one bows. Rather, true

[1] See Mark 16:18.

worship has to do with the heart – before what, before Whom, is it bowed?

Where and in what does one's heart find security, significance, and satisfaction?

As the leadership guru John Maxwell repeatedly insists, "Everything rises or falls on leadership." Typically, as the worship leader, so the congregation. Before proceeding, let's concede an inescapable aspect of performance. Those leading are necessarily "up front."

During a large worship conference I heard the Vineyard songwriter and leader, Kevin Prosch, put the matter succinctly: "Tune or die!" Some other basics are non-negotiable. One hopes that at least the musicians are on same song sheet and playing in the same key. The guys on the soundboard need to have done their job mixing and balancing so there are no heart-stopping squawks and squeals. But thereafter, the question stands: *Are the performance aspects of worship dialed down as close to zero as possible?*

Answering that question requires a ruthless, even a brutal honesty. Once definitively answered, it leaves us forever changed. This I learned from Don Potter. I had the privilege of sharing a platform with Don several years ago. At the time he was partnered with Rick Joyner and Morningstar ministries. Over lunch we talked about some of his earlier professional music days when he played guitar with Chuck Mangione and Bruce Cockburn. He then candidly shared an experience that profoundly marked the contrast. While leading worship at a large conference the Lord spoke to Don very clearly, saying, "You're entertaining. Face the wall and praise Me until you learn to truly sense My presence." Alone in his bedroom, it wasn't long before Don was painfully aware that the songs he had been singing, the "crowd pleasers" as he called them, were not what he was to be singing to his Lord and Master. As he put it, "It had to be something from my heart and every word of it had to be true." Once he felt the Lord's release to lead corporately, Don literally worshiped facing the wall for over six months, his back turned away from the gathered, his focus fixed only on the "audience of One."

While those of us in the congregation do not have to contend with these sorts of performance issues, one of the questions we do have to answer is, whose praise are we singing? I have been in a few situations where it might as well have been framed in stained glass: "In memory of God, to the glory of the band."

It is possible to *worship* worship. And to worship the worship leader. I have been in such intense times of praise that it was completely appropriate to give the Lord a standing ovation. Other times I've almost felt ill as the ones up front received the adulation.

One of the uglier faces of performance is that of competition. Knowing this, it was with some reservation that I invited five worship leaders to join me on a tour of some of the Betel churches in Spain and Portugal. Each of them was a gifted leader in their own right and I wondered how they would function together. One morning we were given a test. We had to wait on our host, Elliott Tepper, as he concluded some urgent business before we could travel several hours to another of Betel's works. To make the best use of our time I suggested that we as ministry team worship together. We sang, prayed, read Scripture and waited in silence. The worship leaders passed a borrowed guitar around as each felt a stirring to lead. It was a most uncommon time of mutual honor, submission and laid-down love, all in offering to the Lord. It was totally unplanned, but long prepared, for there was in these men and women nothing of performance and absolutely nothing of competition. As we worshiped in such purity of heart, the two hours together seemed like only moments. After his long delay, Elliott came running into a room that had become so filled with

the Lord's glorious presence that he literally skidded to a halt,
realizing that he had burst into holy ground.

Competition is often a function of insecurity. In this regard, the
five worship leaders on my team had spent sufficient time alone
with the Lord to get themselves sorted. But it's a process that
many avoid, or at least compromise. There's a great truth in the
business mantra that says, "Five-star people hire five-star people;
three-star people hire two." A leader who is threatened by
another's gifting will exercise Machiavellian tactics to make sure
no one rises above their level of influence. The infamous Italian
Prince held that "Government consists mainly in so keeping your
subjects that they shall be neither able nor disposed to injure you;
and this is done by depriving them of all means of injuring you." [2]
I know of a grievous situation where a very gifted worshiper had
a short tenure on a church's worship team because it quickly
became clear that she outshone the self-appointed "leader." She
was coldly dismissed with the words, "We don't need you at this
time." Not only was she sinned against; the church family was
deprived of the fruits of her anointing.

One of the ways for a worship leader to assess whether or not
there are performance issues at work is to ask, "As I stand up to
lead, is there any adrenalin flowing? Are my knees shaky, my
mouth dry or my palms sweaty?" This may signal the felt need
to impress somebody. It may be a sign that there is yet the
need to earn approval. If so, it marks the time to stand down.
The focus has become misplaced and until it is sorted, any
leadership authority will be compromised.

Again, the contrast is so very marked. The second day of a
large conference in Switzerland, I crossed paths with the back-
up vocalist while in the foyer of the meeting hall. I thanked her
for leading the worship the night before. She got a puzzled look
on her face and, speaking more and more slowly, in English,
she tried to help me understand in my mother tongue that she

[2] Niccolo Machiavelli, *The Prince and the Discourses*, The Modern Library, New
York, 1950, p. 358.

wasn't leading last night – she was singing back-up vocals. "Maurice,[3] on the keyboard, he was leading." Maurice was definitely "up front." But he was also evidently nervous in front of such a large crowd. As Maurice was struggling, I was drawn to this woman singing back-up vocals, because her unaffected worship called forth my worship. Her heart, drawn into the heart of God, drew mine. When she finally understood what I was saying, she broke into a gentle smile and humbly said, "Merci monsieur."

The larger principle at work here is inescapable. *The ones up front do not have any authority to take the gathered to a place they've rarely been to, or worse, never been.*

Another way of addressing the issue is this: *Are the ones up front song leaders or worshipers?*

One of the ways of answering this question is with some further questions: would those up front be doing what they're doing if there was no one else in the building? Are they fussed if only a few people gather to worship with them? Or are they just as content to worship in an empty sanctuary, knowing that the Lord was present long before their arrival?

What we're trying to assess is, for whom are we singing? Conduct an exit eavesdrop some time. Stand just past the doors of church at the close of a service and listen for something of the following: "I didn't like the worship at all this morning. It didn't do anything for me." Such a statement succinctly declares the misunderstood mandate of worship. Is a local church seeking to construct "inspiring and vibrant services of worship"? If so, it is another example of misplaced focus. Those who are quick to complain that they left feeling uninspired need to understand that true worship wasn't *for* them. Was it the worship the *Father* desired? Did He like it?

One of the ways our worship gets compromised is the way in which the recruitment appeal goes out: "We're desperate for a drummer. If you can keep a beat and have a pulse, we need

---

[3] His name has been changed.

you." If that's the case, then as long as a person is warm and willing they can meet a need on the team. But with such an approach there is zero attentiveness or discernment. Those up front may well be capable musicians; that's not the issue. Rather, are they themselves worshipers, and are any of them anointed to lead worship? Too often we've confused talent with authority and mistaken ability for calling.

Most of us would be quick to acknowledge that the pulpit is not a soapbox for anyone who has an opinion, so why do we open worship leadership to anyone who can carry a tune?

More broadly, there is a very quick and easy worship diagnostic: are we singing about God or to God? It is fairly easy to sing, "God is so good." In a worst case scenario an adulterer can come to church with his estranged wife and he can sing, "God is so good." He can do so because he's glad his infidelity hasn't been discovered this week.

The same man cannot sing, "I will give You all my worship – You alone I long to worship" or "Lord, I give You my heart, I give You my soul." That, because true worship in Spirit and in truth necessarily changes us. When our hearts are drawn into the heart of God there is more of His love, more of His grace, more of His holiness revealed, both to us and through us. We cannot worship and stay as we were.

An irreducible evaluation of worship follows: are we leaving a service different people than when we came in? Do we finish up our time of private worship in a different "space" than when we began? As the Apostle Paul prays in Ephesians 3:17, are we more *"rooted and grounded in love"*[4] than when we started?

For instance, one of my regular church hosts asked if I would bring a message titled, "How to hold on to God in troubled times." As I prayed about it, the word became one of worship, because when it's bad enough, for long enough, the only way I

[4] NASB.

can hold on to God in troubled times is to take time, to make the time, such that I know again, that *He's* holding on to me. I had that much of the message established when my wife told me that she had spent two and a half hours listening to one song on her iPod over and over, *Yet I will praise You.* She did so until the truths of that song convinced and transformed her heart, and brought her to a place of peace that *"transcends all understanding."*[5]

I have joked with some of the musicians I know, saying that their worship CDs should come with a printed warning on the wrappers: "Contents proven hazardous to health – even secondhand worship can kill!" Often as I've worshiped, the words of the songs have been used of the Spirit to kill off some more of my flesh and put to death more of my soulish inclinations. If, for instance, we catch ourselves singing, "Refiner's fire, my heart's one desire is to be holy," we ought to recognize that the Father loves to answer that prayer and that the Spirit counts the singing of that song as permission to have at us. We ought to expect to come under conviction about those things that yet need sanctification and redemption in our lives, unto a greater wholeness and holiness in Christ.

Though the Lord's word to Nicodemus is a generic absolute, it can appropriately be applied to corporate worship: *"Flesh gives birth to flesh, but the Spirit gives birth to spirit"* (John 3:6 NIV). As one in the congregation there are services I've endured where we've finished up the sing-song and then bopped into announcements, sat through the "chat," and then headed home unmoved and unchanged, struggling to silence the inclination to criticize and find fault. At the other end of the continuum there are times when we've worshiped in Spirit and in truth, and sensed that the place we've come to has become holy ground. After an uncommonly profound worship time at St Aldates, Oxford, for instance, I was so humbled I removed

[5] Philippians 4:7, NIV.

my shoes and preached in my sock feet. It was not something that I alone felt – the ministry time afterwards was one of the most holy and consecrated I have ever experienced.

There are other times when it seems that the song leader has charged through the set as if they were glad to get it over with for another week. But the mandate for a worship leader is to make space and place for us to attend to the work of the Spirit of God in our midst. Through the course of the worship there ought to be the opportunity for us to empty ourselves of all our worries, anxieties and fears, to confess our anger, resentment and bitterness; to repent of our failures and compromises. In this emptying, we "[cast] *all our cares on him*" (1 Peter 5:7 NET) and unburden ourselves of all we're trying to hang onto, or can't let go of. Privately, one of the songs that is near the top of my worship playlist is Craig Musseau's *Pour out my heart*: "Here I am, once again. I pour out my heart for I know that You hear every cry . . ." One of the reasons that it's a favorite is that it's sung in a blues key. Truth to tell, that's often where my worship begins.

It's not where it ends however, because after the emptying comes the filling. It is our Lord's heart to *"give grace to the humble"* (1 Peter 5:5 NIV). As we pour out our hearts, releasing all to His care and keeping, He is ever faithful to impart to us yet again – more of Christ's righteousness, His peace, love, joy, revealed anew. That's why we finish up worshiping as different people.

There are some church families that are not used to physical demonstrations during worship. In these situations I'm often asked why I raise my arms in such abandon. I explain that it's the outward sign of the inward grace that's been received, for I've been brought to a place of unconditional surrender. As a student of both the Scriptures and the history of the Church, I know that there are no accounts of anyone fighting God and winning. My raised arms are the recognition that I won't be the first. More, I'm convinced that I do not want anything God doesn't want me to have. Nor do I want to spend any effort trying to convince Him otherwise.

In Zechariah 2:13 we read *"Let all mortals be silent in the presence of the LORD! For he has bestirred himself and come out from his holy dwelling place."* The prophet is using metaphoric language here, for there is no place God isn't, and when He stirs it's not that He's been asleep. Rather, as He moves, something in us is stirred ... called ... convicted. And when the Lord is on the move it's for us to attend to where He's heading, for in true worship we are ever the ones following.

In the broadest of terms I understand worship as the aligning of our hearts and our heart's affections with the Lord's. In the opening of Mark's Gospel Jesus says, *"The Kingdom of God is upon you. Repent and believe"* (Mark 1:15). The word "repentance" in Greek is *metanoia*. It is a compound word derived from *meta*, "around," and *nous*, "mind." Literally, repentance means "change the way you think." It could rightly be paraphrased, "See things the way God sees them." True worship brings us to the place where all that is in us says to the Lord the best "yes" we can, our hearts aligned with His.

(If we're saying "maybe" we're dithering, and if there's a "no" in our spirits, we're still in rebellion.)

Hebrews 4:12 reads *"The word of God is alive and active. It cuts more keenly than any two-edged sword, piercing so deeply that it divides soul and spirit, joints and marrow; it discriminates among the thoughts and purposes of the heart."* That's why we finish true worship as changed people. So much of what we sing, when we sing to God, is taken from Scripture. Declaring His Word personally means that we can't stay the way we were before we started. We get pierced and the affections of our hearts get divided as we go "under the knife." The Divine Physician cuts away that which is yet diseased and we are then healthier, holier and happier.

With chagrin, I confess that I have not always understood

worship so dynamically. As a young preacher I used to consider "worship" as the preliminary that all too often ate into the preach. That had me frequently at loggerheads with the church organist. The service could only last an hour and so she had twenty minutes and not a minute more. If she slotted in four hymns on a given Sunday then that meant we'd have to cut verses out in order to make up time. I now recognize that it is as incongruous to engage in a "bit of worship" as it is to speak a "bit of a preach." I have become a worshiper and my worship is so much more than Sunday's allotted time.

This then poses the diagnostic questions:

How much of life, both the church's corporate life, and our personal lives, is characterized by worship, beyond the Sunday gathering?

How ongoing and habitual is the aligning of our hearts and our hearts' affections?

The scriptures are replete with glorious bursts of praise: *"Sing for joy, O heavens ... shout aloud, earth beneath"* (Isaiah 44:23 NIV). Seraphim and cherubim are admonished to sing in unbroken song: *"Praise him, all his angels; praise him, all his heavenly hosts"* (Psalm 148:2 NIV). All creation sings: *"Praise him, sun and moon; praise him, all you shining stars"* (Psalm 148:3 NIV); *"Mountains and hills will break forth into shouts for joy before you, and all the trees of the field will clap their hands"* (Isaiah 55:12 NASB).

In *Worship, The Missing Jewel of the Evangelical Church*, A.W. Tozer graphically contrasts creation's worship and our inclinations towards self-preoccupation: "All else fulfills its design; flowers are still fragrant ... birds still sing with their thousand voice choir on a summer's day, and the sun and the moon and the stars all move on their rounds doing the will of God ... Man alone sulks in his cave."[6]

With all the gifts that we've been given, all the grace, all the blessings – and while all the rest of creation bursts with praise – we alone sulk in our caves.

[6] A.W. Tozer, *Worship, The Missing Jewel of the Evangelical Church*, Christian Publications, Pennsylvania, 1961, p. 11.

Many of us are hard pressed and some readers may be thinking, "You don't know what my life is like." But we are not called to praise only when things are free and breezy. After calling us to *"pray continually,"* the apostle Paul adds, *"give thanks whatever happens"* (1 Thessalonians 5:17–18). The NIV translates the last phrase *"in all circumstances."* How can Paul give thanks "in all things"? How can we?

While working on this material I was the victim of a smash and grab in which I had my laptop bag stolen. I lost not only my computer, but my digital camera, my iPod and headphones, several hundred dollars of cash, my passport and all my ID. When we returned to my host's van and discovered the theft, I didn't swear, not even in my head. I had preached the night before and had finished with the simple prayer, "Father, I receive the grace You have for me this day." Standing in the midst of the broken glass from the smashed window, I rehearsed that prayer several times.

If, in spite of contrary providences, ours is an unshakeable confidence that God is for us and not against us, we can give thanks whatever happens. In spite of desperate circumstances it is ours to trust that God is nevertheless working larger kingdom purposes in the midst of things. After we'd finished with the police report, I looked out over a beautiful Surrey valley and said out loud, "Lord, I'm really looking forward to seeing how You're going to redeem this mess."

I was standing on ground that had previously been taken. The apostle asks a rhetorical question in Romans 8: *"What can separate us from the love of Christ?"* He then puts forward a fairly comprehensive list: *"Can affliction or hardship? Can persecution, hunger, danger, or sword?"* (Romans 8:35). Some of those to whom Paul was writing had lost friends and family to a martyr's death. In comparison, the theft of my personals was trivial, inconvenient at worst. Nevertheless, it could have spun my little world out of orbit. I trust that with Paul, I have it settled: *"I am convinced that there is nothing in death or life, in the realm of spirits or superhuman powers, in the world as it is or the world as it shall be, in the forces of the universe, in heights or depths – nothing in all creation that can separate us from the love of God in Christ Jesus our Lord."*

The only way our hearts and hearts' affections can be so assured is through a life of worship. If we can rest in the knowledge of God's unfailing love, then we can prevail over the aggravation of our present circumstances. As we choose to align our hearts and hearts' affections with His we are then affirming greater faith in God's faithfulness than faith in our present understanding of the challenging circumstances we face.

True worship is a grace, a gift given. In 2 Thessalonians 3:5 Paul prays, *"May the Lord direct your hearts towards God's love and the steadfastness of Christ."* Grammatically this is not an imperative, something we have to do. We are not required to try to direct our hearts towards God's. It is both God's work and His desire to draw our hearts' desires into His love. As the Church father Bernard of Clairvaux said 900 years ago,

> "[God] is both the prime mover of our love and final end ... His love both opens up the way for ours and is our love's reward ... Every soul among you that is seeking God should know that it has been anticipated by Him, and has been sought by Him before it began to seek Him."[7]

If it were possible, the second phrase, *"the steadfastness of Christ"* is even more compelling. Of all the things in which Jesus was steadfast He was most constant in His unbroken communion with His Father. He was not just "with" the Father; in John 10:38 He says to the Jews that had gathered around Him, *"Know that the Father is in me, and I in the Father."*

As we worship, we are drawn into that same intimate union. In Ephesians Paul states that by the grace of God we have been

---

[7] Bernard of Claivaux, "On the Love of God," and "That the Soul, Seeking God, is Anticipated by Him," *Late Medieval Mysticism*, ed. Ray Petry, Westminster Press, Philadelphia, 1957, pp. 59, 75.

brought to life with Christ. He then says that we are not only saved from our sin, but that God, *"raised us up in union with Christ Jesus and enthroned us with him in the heavenly realms, so that he might display in the ages to come how immense are the resources of his grace, and how great his kindness to us in Christ Jesus."* All, *"because of his great love for us"* (Ephesians 2:6, 4). Our enthronement with Christ is more about identity and relationship than it is about position or location, or even power and authority.

I was recently with a church where this became very evident. There is a great deal of truth in the philosophic declaration that "language defines reality." The words we use and the ways in which we use them define how and what we think and believe. The church I was with was a liturgical church. At the formal Sunday morning service they led the worship and the prayers, and I preached. Over lunch I asked one of the pastors to close his eyes and attend to the gut, visceral answer that my forthcoming question evoked.

I asked, "As you work through the liturgy, do you understand yourself to be a sinner who struggles to love God, or are you a lover of God who sometimes struggles with sin?"

There was but a moment's pause and the pastor exclaimed, "Oh my!" What followed was a long and extended conversation about primary identity and relationship. Along the way I referenced Cranmer's confession. Thomas Cranmer is considered the great architect of Anglican theology. He was not just a thinker, however, for so passionate was his faith that he was willing to endure a martyr's death. Many readers will have some familiarity with Cranmer's magnificent prose as found in the Book of Common Prayer.

His morning confession, while it rolls off the tongue, is a prayer for those who know themselves to be sinners who struggle to love God. At seminary, we referred to it as "worm theology" that had us groveling before a faultfinding God. The confession reads:

Almighty and most merciful Father, we have erred and strayed from thy ways like lost sheep, we have followed too much the devices and desires of our own hearts, we have offended against thy holy laws, we have left undone those things which we ought to have done, and we have done those things which we ought not to have done; and there is no health in us. But thou, O Lord, have mercy upon us, miserable offenders . . . .[8]

As a declaration of primary identity, Cranmer's confession concisely defines the mess we've made of things as pre-converted sinners, whether or not we're struggling to love God. In Christ, however, we are no longer "miserable offenders." We have confessed our sins and should be assured that we have been forgiven and cleansed of all our unrighteousness (1 John 1:9). We are justified in Christ and are in the process of being sanctified. The language of Cranmer's liturgy defines an inferior reality, for *"there is now no condemnation for those who are united with Christ Jesus"* (Romans 8:1). While we continue to struggle with sin and need to make ongoing confession, our primary identity is not that we are failing sinners. We are more than forgiven sinners. Our Heavenly Father sees us as His beloved sons and daughters. Drawn into the heart of God and the steadfastness of Christ, if we see things the way God sees them we are to understand ourselves to be lovers more than we are miserable offenders.

The life of a sinner struggling to love God is a heroic effort to try to get it right. Worship as such is often a duty. It almost ought to be as boring as possible as the penance for our failures. In such twisted thinking the tedium must be endured before there can be absolution.

In contrast, life as a lover of God is the celebration of a graced self-understanding. Worship is embraced as our communion

---

[8] *Book of Common Prayer*, University Press, Cambridge, 1962, "Morning Prayer," p. 5.

with the One who loves us more than we love ourselves. It is life with the One who receives us unconditionally, regardless of how we've lived out the challenges we face.

The apostle Peter declares, *"[God] has given us his promises . . . so that . . . we may share in the divine nature"* (2 Peter 1:4). The word "share" is the translation of *koinonos*, a derivative of *koinonia*. Using the same root word, the apostle John declares his reason for writing – *"that you may share with us in a common life, that life which we share with the Father and his Son Jesus Christ"* (1 John 1:3). Later he will state that, *"God is love"* (1 John 4:8) and will go to great lengths to describe what our relationships in that love will look like.

Similarly, Jude writes *". . . to those whom God has called, who live in the love of God the Father"* (Jude 1). The NRSV translates the objective phrase as *"beloved in God the Father,"* the NET Bible, *"those . . . wrapped in the love of God the Father."* However it's expressed, the verb tense is a perfect passive participle. We ought therefore to understand that we have been loved, are now loved, yet will be loved, whether we want to be or not!

A few verses later, Jude names the counterpoint to the passive participle used in verse 1, for he admonishes his friends to *"keep* [them]*selves in the love of God"* (Jude 21). Here the verb tense is aorist, active, imperative. Our response to the love with which we are loved is to actively and continuously rejoice in and nurture that love. It is to declare our "Yes" to the love in which we are wrapped. It is to rehearse our "Thank you", our "More, please."

It is to become worshipers *"in Spirit and in truth"* and so fulfill the Father's desire (John 4:23).

There is for each of us a defining moment when we say our first "Yes" to God. It marks our passage from darkness to light, from estrangement to communion, from rebellion to obedience. But it is the first yes in a new life of agreement with the Lord. In this regard the aligning of our hearts is not unlike a transatlantic flight. I quite regularly take off from Toronto Pearson International Airport bound for London Heathrow. While we track a well-defined great circle route there are innumerable mid-course corrections that need to be made as our course is compromised by fluctuations in the Jet Stream.

While our spiritual journey is also well defined, it is not casually achieved. All manner of forces, from all manner of directions, continuously challenge our progress. Only a life of worship keeps us heading in the right direction as we respond to the work of the Spirit attentively guiding, redirecting and empowering us. We have God's promise: *"If you stray from the path, whether to the right or to the left, you will hear a voice from behind you sounding in your ears saying, 'This is the way; follow it' "* (Isaiah 30:21). The Spirit doesn't just intervene when we're in danger of heading out of bounds, however. Jesus spoke of the Revealer's fuller work: *"When the Spirit of Truth comes, he will guide you into all the truth . . . and he will make known to you what is to come. He will glorify me, for he will take what is mine and make it known to you"* (John 16:13–14).

Worship in Spirit and truth, seeing things as God sees them, attentiveness, alignment of heart, restoration and redemption, direction and revelation, may seem too much to hope for in a single service of worship. We're certainly left forever changed should we experience such holy glory. Though I told the story briefly in my book *Turnings*, the following encounter is unquestionably one of my defining moments of worship, and as such, I can do no better than retell it.

In February 2000 I was with my dear friends of Betel, in Madrid, Spain. The majority of the thousand-plus gathered had been gloriously saved from the depths of heroin addiction. Betel is one of the most missional churches I know of and the church is continuously caring for new guys in off the streets.

As I waited on the Lord while preparing for the Sunday morning service, I sensed the Spirit stirring my spirit with the conviction that I was to call in the lost before I preached. The sense was so strong I went to church with heightened expectations.

Our worship that morning was as passionate and pure as it typically is at Betel. There was nothing of performance or competition; rather, men and women with broken bodies and redeemed spirits declared their thanks and praise. Tattooed arms were raised in surrender and abandon. Previously hard and desperate lives were now tender and humble.

The last song in the opening worship set was *Ven, Espiritu, Ven*. It is a prayer of petition: "Come, Spirit, come: come and fill my life. Cleanse me and wash me; renew me, and restore me with your power. I want to know you."

While we were singing the chorus for the last time, I heard in my spirit the Spirit say, "Now!" As soon as we finished singing, I walked up to the platform and said, "If that's your prayer – if you want the Spirit of God to come and cleanse you, renew you and restore you, and you're never asked Jesus to be your Savior, come and receive the cleansing that His love brings. The peace that you sense, the joy that you see on the faces around you, the love that you've experienced from the community here – all of that is what life filled with the Holy Spirit is like. If that's what you want, cleansing, peace, joy, love, come." Within minutes, there were sixty guys at the front of the church. I asked the Betel pastors to come forward as well, and together we prayed with these men who'd been drawn into the love of God.

2

Leadership Priorities

The term "church growth" is a large and sloppy one. Out of curiosity, I Googled "church growth resources." Nanoseconds later I was inundated with 2,140,000 results! Though I scanned only the first few pages, what stood out beyond the denominational and network links were the adverts: "Dramatic Church Growth: Double your church attendance in 90 days. Simple, low-cost program;" "Church Growth Advice: Church websites can draw in non-Christians to your church;" "Church not growing? Even shrinking? Find a brand new approach!"

This cursory search confirmed my conviction that one needs to ask ruthless questions of church growth. Specifically, *what* is growing? If one works the metaphor it is possible to grow church mushrooms quite quickly and easily. In contrast, the Isaiah 61:3 *"oaks of righteousness"* are raised up very differently. Without engaging in a discourse on end-time theology, my studies assure me that things are going to get far worse before they get better. Mushrooms will certainly not stand or be able to withstand persecution and martyrdom. But it doesn't take the apocalypse to tell the difference. When present day-to-day trials and sufferings have to be endured, oaks of righteousness prevail in ways that mushrooms cannot. Under duress, a well-versed mushroom may pray from John 12:27, *"Father, save me from this hour."* An oak, by way of contrast, is not worried about personal safety and security. Convinced of the sovereign and providential care of their heavenly Father, oaks offer up a far greater petition. In the midst of tribulation, they pray from the latter half of the same verse: *"Father, glorify your name."*

Not every numerically growing church is a qualitatively healthy church. A church can be well attended, but for all the wrong reasons. A healthy church, in contrast, must necessarily be growing; there will be both deepening spiritual maturity and conversions; discipleship and evangelism will be evident.

✛ ✛ ✛

As a diagnostician, the second vital sign I try to discern is how senior leaders spend their time. What are their priorities? Where and on what do they spend their energy? The answers to these questions are fundamental to the healthy growth of the church.

It is a hard truth, but in life and in ministry especially, we're going to disappoint somebody. A church leader faces too many demands. It's too big a job because the needs are endless. A ruthless decision is required: who are we going to disappoint? We can't spend time with everybody.

I asked a huge-hearted, loving pastor about the time he spent in counseling. He responded with a look of shock on his face; his reaction surprised me. Moments later we both burst into laughter. I rephrased my question: "How much time do you spend counseling folks?" He reckoned that in any given week he spent between fourteen and twenty-five hours, somewhere from a third to a half of his workweek. In telling this story, I am in no way faulting either this pastor or the ministry of counseling. What I was asking after was his primary call. If senior leaders spend more than six to eight hours a week counseling, they have compromised the authority of their leadership of the local church.

A responsible pastor lives with the constant tension that there is too much to do and not enough time to do it in. Without constant diligence, priorities quickly get skewed. I put it to my friend that he had to discern his gifting and call. If it was counseling, then he needed to resign as senior pastor and devote himself to his passion. If he and the church believed that indeed he was called to senior leadership, then he needed to recognize that the counseling hours he was spending were eating into too much of the time that needed to be spent elsewhere. (He is assured of his pastoral calling and subsequently rearranged his priorities.)

Shortly after that encounter I met with a young pastor who was run ragged spinning plates. Though the church was only recently planted, it had grown to almost a thousand within its first year. I listened as he told me about all the challenges he was facing and then asked, "Are you spending more time on administration or sermon preparation?" I anticipated his answer. Again I raised the question of calling and gifting. There was no dispute that the church desperately needed a full-time administrator. But the church had a greater need to hear the Word of God preached with authority. Which was my friend's calling?

I rehearsed Acts 6:1, *"when the disciples were growing in number"* the priority of the senior leaders was established: a non-negotiable, uncompromised devotion to *"prayer and to the ministry of the Word"* (Acts 6:4). I asked this pastor how much regular, disciplined time he spent alone with God. He literally hung his head and wearily confessed, "Not nearly enough."

I recently preached at my home church and the primacy of time alone with God was yet again re-enforced. The text that I was studying was from John 14. I was suddenly taken with the Lord's statement: *"I am not myself the source of the words I speak to you: it is the Father who dwells in me doing his own work"* (John 14:10b). As I was working on Sunday's sermon that gave me pause, for if Jesus was not the source of the words He spoke, I certainly didn't want to be the source of the words I was preparing for Sunday's message. From there my thoughts slid laterally and I did a word study on "nothing," *oudeis*, in the Gospel of John.

The ex-blind man testifies to the Pharisees about his healing stating, *"If this man [Jesus] was not from God he could do nothing"* (John 10:33). John the Baptist declares, *"A man can receive nothing, except it be given him from heaven"* (John 3:27 KJV).

Jesus used the word repeatedly:

> *"The Son can do nothing by himself; he does only what he sees the Father doing."*
>
> (John 5:19)

> *"By myself I can do nothing . . . I seek only the will of the One who sent me."*
>
> (John 5:30)

> *"It is the Spirit that gives life; the flesh can achieve nothing."*
>
> (John 6:63)

> *"I do nothing on my own authority, but in all I say, I have been taught by my Father."*
>
> (John 8:28)

> *"Anyone who dwells in me, as I dwell in him, bears much fruit. Apart from me you can do nothing."*
>
> (John 15:5)

Lest things be misconstrued, this is not license to do "nothing." Several years ago, I preached at a church weekend that was hosted by a man who was trying to serve well beyond his gifting. Over the course of our three days together it was obvious on numerous counts that he was failing in his capacity as a pastor. At one point in our conversations he proudly declared that he spent his weekday afternoons "soaking." He would put on a worship CD, lie on the couch and "wait on the Lord." He then said, "It was such a relief when I heard it was OK if I fall asleep while soaking." After a moment's silent prayer I felt I received the Lord's permission to reply, "Mate, you're not soaking, you're having an afternoon nap." I then detailed some of the ways in which he was abdicating his responsibilities by checking out for several hours a day in the name of soaking.

Prayer and study is hard work. It requires discipline. It is far easier to fill that time with all manner of other things. And because many of us are inclined to be lazy, we stay busy, rather than apply ourselves to the real work we are called to do. It is easier to give the urgent precedence over the vital.

While speaking along these lines I asked the gathered at a clergy afternoon workshop, "Do you spend more time on Sunday's PowerPoint presentation than you do in prayer?" An awkward silence followed. A PowerPoint that sings and dances takes a lot of time to prepare. But if it's a significant chunk of the workweek, when does the preacher make the time and space to hear what the Spirit is saying to the church? Rehearsing what one has heard at the most recent conference, or on somebody else's CD, or read on an internet sermon isn't good enough. Revelation comes only through time alone with God. Anything short of it is just blahdy-blah, and yakking in the name of Jesus doesn't raise up the oaks of righteousness.

If, or once, senior leadership accepts that prayer and the study of the Word is their primary calling, questions of appropriation need to be asked. How guarded is that priority? How is it honored, respected and cherished? These questions need to be answered first by senior leadership and then by supporting staff.

While I was pastor of First Baptist Church, Niagara Falls, I was blessed with Lola "the wonder secretary." Among her many gifts she was perhaps the most detailed and organized person I've ever met and I was thrilled to let her strategically run my work life. Once I established the parameters of my prayer and study time with her, she guarded it ruthlessly. If, during that time, someone called the church office wanting to speak to me, she would answer, truthfully, "He's with Someone right now. May I help you?" Over the years it became obvious that Lola was far more gifted pastorally than I was and she essentially became my associate pastor. Often Lola's intervention meant many folks never got to me, and all in, they were glad!

Once staff are allies in the management of priorities, the congregation also needs to understand and respect the senior's primary calling to prayer and the study of the Word. Among other things, it determines when and how they contact him. Do they try to ring him during his prayer time, knowing that they'll get him in? If so, they are not-so-subtly sabotaging his ministry. Instead, they could be encouraged to email him with their concerns, assured that he checks his email once his prayer and study time is concluded.

Just as the first chapter was not just about worship leaders, so the focus here is broader than just preachers. For any one of us to give significant leadership in our sphere of influence we need to know the heart and timely purposes of God for our own lives, our families and church families, and our communities. In this regard, it serves to employ the term "quality time." Typically it applies to parenting and marriage. More than anything else, the effort we spend attentively listening to our children and our spouse directly affects the health and wellbeing of our relationships. If we don't spend quality time with those near and dear to us, there are dire consequences. So too with the Lord. The Scriptures repeatedly sound both the warning, *"Because they have not listened to* [the Lord] *they will become wanderers"* (Hosea 9:17) and the call, *"O that you would listen to him today"* (Hebrews 3:7 NRSV).

Personally, a twenty minute quiet time is not nearly adequate. It takes at least that long to settle myself and clear the decks of the day's flotsam and jetsam. Though I've been working at it for over thirty years, it continues to take considerable time to still my heart and mind, and to silence all the other inner voices that clamor for attention.

For a season, a gallon jar sat on my desk as a reminder. I had put several handfuls of mud into the jar and then filled it with water. A good shaking swirled things such that it was a murky mess. The longer it then sat undisturbed, the clearer it became. I have it established: lasting clarity never comes quickly. Only a priority commitment to time alone with God keeps me from traveling at ninety miles an hour through an interior wasteland.

The quieting in the quiet time is just the preliminary phase. Thereafter, we must give God time to work, for just as in worship, a filling typically follows the emptying, the increase after the decrease (see John 3:30). One of my favorite writers, the Trappist monk, Thomas Merton, reflected:

> True encounter with Christ in the Word of God awakens something in the depth of our being, something we did not know was there. True encounter with Christ liberates something in us, a power we did not know we had; a hope, a capacity for life, a resilience, an ability to bounce back when we thought we were completely defeated, a capacity to grow, and change, a power of creative transformation.[1]

Time and time again, I am often well into an hour's prayer time before that ability to bounce back is restored within. If I compromise that time, I feel ill-equipped to head back into the fray.

Regardless of translation, the term "quality time" will not be found in any Bible. Meditation, however, may be considered a close equivalent. The call to meditation is one of the hallmarks of the Psalms. The one blessed of the Lord, *"meditates* [on the law of the Lord] *day and night"* (Psalm 1:2 NIV). The faithful *"meditate on* [the Lord's] *unfailing love"* (Psalm 48:9). When in despair, the psalmist says, *"I will remember the deeds of the* LORD; *yes, I remember your miracles of long ago; I meditate on all your*

[1]   Thomas Merton, *He Is Risen*, Argus Communications, Niles, Il., 1975, p. 15.

works" (Psalm 77:11–12 NIV). The Psalmist meditates on the Lord's precepts, His statutes and His wonders, His decrees and His promises (Psalm 119:15, 23, 27, 48, 148).

Some readers may be unhinged at the thought of Christians meditating. Isn't that what Buddhists do? Didn't Jesus say, *"In your prayers do not go babbling on like the heathen . . . Do not imitate them . . . "* (Matthew 6:7–8a)? The babbling Jesus refers to is not the meditation the Psalmist calls forth. The heathen have no relationship with God. They do not know the One they're talking to. Nor do they know what the words they use mean. They may not be attempting to talk to anybody at all, for it is possible to use the techniques of meditation without any belief system. Jesus explicitly names the contrast: *"Your Father knows what your needs are before you ask him"* (Matthew 6:8b).

For many, that declaration begs the questions, "Why then do we pray? If God knows my needs, why spend time and effort telling Him what he already knows?"

The answer is, ultimately, we don't. We don't pray in order to keep an omniscient being in the loop. Our heavenly Father already knows our needs. In fact, He knows our hearts and hearts' affections better than we do. The reason we pray is to know what's on *His* heart.

Two Hebrew words are translated as "meditate." One means to "to mutter or mumble," the other, "to bow down." Both are word pictures. Meditation on the Scriptures is a super-slow reading and re-reading of phrases or sentences, as though we were simmering the Scriptures, all the while asking the Spirit to take those words deep into our hearts and bring further, fuller revelation. It is one of the ways the apostle Paul's prayer is answered, *"that the God of our Lord Jesus Christ, the all-glorious Father, may confer on you the spiritual gifts of wisdom and vision, with the knowledge of him that they bring"* (Ephesians 1:17).

Over the last few weeks I have been muttering and mumbling Jude 2, *"Mercy, peace, and love be yours in fullest measure."* I have sat for hours with that verse and taken it for long walks. I have given thanks for the mercy, peace and love that I have already received. I have marveled at the ways in which the mercy, peace and love of God have redeemed and sustained my life. I have reflected on those areas of my life that yet need to be transformed by mercy, peace and love, and have bowed in submission as the Spirit has brought further conviction and consecration. I have wondered about the increase, the *fullest measure*, or, as it is translated elsewhere, the *"abundance"* (NIV). What does it mean for my life if mercy, peace and love are further *"multiplied"* (KJV)?

In all of this, meditation involves a deliberate un-tethering from all that entangles, intentionally withdrawing from all the pushing and shoving that takes place in the living of life. Once a measure of stillness is managed, one then has a greater freedom to attend to the Spirit's call, His leading and guiding, and this always opens to us more of the abundant life that is ours in Christ.

In Galatians 6:7 Paul writes, *"Do not be deceived."* That's the way the NIV translates the phrase. The word for deception could also be rendered, "led astray, or wander about." However it's expressed, it's a warning. If unawares, we can easily be deceived. Without attention we can wander so far that we find ourselves like the prodigal, in a very distant country.

Sin warps our souls over time. Often the real seriousness of our failings is not immediate. Like a cut that gets infected, the initial injury is not as serious as that which festers after the fact. The apostle uses a farming metaphor: *"If* [a man] *sows in the field of his unspiritual nature, he will reap from it a harvest of corruption"* (Galatians 6:8a). Such is the subtlety of sin.

The good news is that in Christ there is the potential for a greater, more abundant harvest. *"If* [a man] *sows in the field of the Spirit, he will reap from it a harvest of eternal life"* (Galatians 6:8b). Paul would have us understand that just as a hard-working farmer intentionally sows good seed, so we are to sow in the Spirit. A harvest of *"love, joy, peace, patience, kindness, goodness, fidelity, gentleness, and self-control"* is not automatic (Galatians 5:22). These godly character traits are formed within us only as we are *"led by the Spirit"* (Galatians 5:18). Thus, *"if the Spirit is the source of our life,* [we are to] *let the Spirit also direct its course"* (Galatians 5:25). Grammatically, the apostle uses present tense verbs when he speaks of being led and directed by the Spirit. This implies that the Spirit is actively guiding and leading. The NIV dynamically renders the passage, *"let us keep in step with the Spirit."*

As we spend time alone with God, our self-centered and self-concerned attitudes shift. But for most of us, most of the time, it's rare that this occurs easily or painlessly, hence the dire warning that Moses received: *"No mortal may see* [the face of God] *and live"* (Exodus 33:20). We cannot come into the presence of God and continue to pray, *"My* will be done ... in Jesus' name." It was *"in anguish of spirit"* that Jesus prayed, *"not my will but yours be done"* (Luke 22:43). There are times and seasons when we too agonize as our soulish desires are brought before the cross for crucifixion, but it is only there that we can come to the purity of heart and the Spirit-controlled abandon that cries, "Holy is *Your* name ... Your Kingdom come, Your will be done."

One of the differences between church mushrooms and oaks of righteousness is that mushrooms believe that God exists to meet their needs. Oaks believe that they exist to seek first the kingdom of heaven. On an ongoing basis, therefore, one of the ways of discerning whether or not we're being led by the Spirit is to ask, *do we have God on our terms, or does He have us on His?*

The discipline of meditation is vital to our spiritual growth and health not because it affords us the space to ask big questions of God, but because it allows God to ask big questions of us. The ways in which we answer determines the course of our lives.

There are no short cuts. Extended time alone in the secret

place cannot be compromised. It is the only source of intimacy, vitality and authority. Ultimately, we spend quality time with the Lord not so that we can achieve something, but that we can be the men and women we are called to be; to know who, and whose, we are. Out of the fullness of our relationship with our Creator and Redeemer then flows the authority to be about the work of His kingdom.

After prayer and study, the next priority of vital leadership is that of discipling, equipping and mentoring. It is, in essence, reproducing leaders. At the outset of Jesus' ministry, *"he appointed twelve . . . that they might be with him and that he might send them out to preach and to have authority to drive out demons"* (Mark 3:14–15 NIV). The apostle Paul wrote to Timothy saying, *"You heard my teaching in the presence of many witnesses; hand on that teaching to reliable men who in turn will be qualified to teach others"* (2 Timothy 2:2).

Few church leaders would dispute this priority in theory. Regrettably, there are many churches where the practice is suspect. Ruthless soul-searching is required: how does the senior leader understand his or her calling? *Is he expecting or requiring that his leaders serve his vision, or is he serving theirs?*

If it's the first, then worst case, the pastor is continuously trying to calculate what he can get out of the flock. When someone new begins attending, it's as if the pastor runs a mental "gifts inventory" in his head and figures out what present need the newcomer can meet.

There is another way. Discernment, not calculation is required. How can the pastor encourage and enable what the Lord is calling forth from each of those entrusted to his care and oversight?

The actual differences in orientation are rarely so extreme. As the issues are subtle, let them be addressed from another angle: is the senior leader raising up for himself devoted followers or empowered leaders? *Which way up is the leadership pyramid?* If the senior leader sees himself as the church's CEO, the leadership pyramid is point up. The message from the top is clearly and unapologetically, "Serve my vision." When things are most unhealthy, support leadership aren't leadership at all. They are compliant drones – "yes" men and women.

While a church may grow quickly and have a great deal of vitality in the early years of ministry, it isn't long before things become toxic and the carnage devastating. Church mushrooms do not have a long shelf life.

The vital life of the kingdom of God requires a flipping of the leadership pyramid. Jesus made this explicit: *"You know that, among the Gentiles, rulers lord it over their subjects, and the great make their authority felt. It shall not be so with you . . . The Son of Man did not come to be served but to serve, and to give his life as a ransom for many"* (Matthew 20:25–28). The healthiest leadership team I've ever encountered was Mike Bickle's when he was the senior pastor of Metro Fellowship in Kansas City. It is an understatement to say that Mike himself was committed to spending time alone with God – he subsequently resigned from Metro's leadership to found and direct the 24/7 International House of Prayer. While he was pastor he gathered around him the strongest team of gifted and anointed peers he could find. As I witnessed their leadership meetings, it was clear that one of their guiding principles was from Proverbs 27:17, *"Iron sharpens iron, so one man sharpens another"* (NIV). They lived out their own amplified version: "Let the sparks fly."

Mike told me that if, at the end of an animated meeting, the team was not in agreement, he would conclude by calling a fast until next week's meeting. If there wasn't agreement then, they fasted another week, and again if needs be, until somebody said something like, "Please forgive me, I've been way out of line. I was pushing my own agenda and timetable. What you guys have been saying is from the Lord. You were right." Sometimes, that would be Mike's confession.

This inverted leadership pyramid is but one of the many kingdom paradoxes that makes the Church a supernatural enterprise. The apostle Paul repeatedly spoke of himself as the Church's servant. This was not conventional rhetoric, but the spirit of his ministry: *"I long to see you so that I may impart to you some spiritual gift to make you strong"* (Romans 1:11 NIV).

I learned this early in the course of my ministry. While I was the pastor of First Baptist, Niagara Falls, Lola set up appointments so that I could meet individually with my senior leaders once a month. The general question that directed our time together was how I could serve them in answer to what it was that they sensed the Lord was calling forth from them. I tried my best to try to equip and enable them.

Our Sunday School superintendent was a woman named Fay. At one of our monthly meetings I asked her, "If you could do anything you wanted for the kingdom of God, what would it be and what would it take?" She had an immediate answer. "I'd put together a summer tutoring program for my kids." I was confused; our Sunday School program wasn't so intense that kids needed that kind of help. Then it dawned on me – Fay was speaking about her kids at "school" school. During the work-week she was the department head of the special needs program at one of our local middle schools. She explained: "My kids can't take the summer off and retain what they have learned from the school year. It's as if we have to start all over again in September. If someone would spend even half an hour a couple of times a week – turning flash cards and reading with them – they could maintain their math and literacy skills and we could make some progress come the following year." Within half an hour, "Kid's Place" was as good as up and running.

We solicited some of our seniors as tutors. Though most of them were reticent about the whole project, it wasn't long before their one-on-one time with the same child became the highlight of their week. Over the six weeks of the summer, these seniors became surrogate grandparents. The children loved the attention they were getting and the parents were thrilled with the kids' new love for learning.

At the end of August we threw a pizza party for the children, the parents and the tutors. We thanked the parents for trusting us with their children and we explained why we offered the program: "We figured that it's what Jesus would do with your child if He were here."

At the start of the new school year the kids asked if Kid's Place couldn't continue. The seniors were thrilled with the request. The numbers, both students and tutors, more than doubled within that first year, and when the children were tested at the end of the second summer, several of them had made so much progress that they were reintegrated into the general school stream. The Board of Education was so impressed with the stories they were hearing about Kid's Place that they offered free resources.

Let it be clearly stated: never in my most creative or inspired moment could I have ever imagined, let alone designed and implemented, Kid's Place. As the senior leader of the church, it was mine to ask Fay, "What do you need and how can I help?"

While I'm trying to get a sense of a senior leader's priorities, I'm also assessing issues of authority, government and oversight. How does this pastor operate? Is he a lone ranger? CEO? Prophetic pioneer? I've been with several leaders who unashamedly name themselves "benevolent dictators." One can only hope they stay benevolent.

The issue here is that of control. It is yet another way of looking at the leadership pyramid. A number of questions follow. With whom is he or she in relationship? Who's speaking into their lives? Certain ministry streams and pastors pride themselves on autonomy and independence. I personally do not know of an independent church that hasn't run into serious problems within a decade. They may be relatively healthy during their infancy as a church, but because there is no one alongside to bring correction and discipline to bear, that lack takes its toll over the years.

Longevity is often a telling measure of health. How long have church staff been employed? How frequent is the turnover? How happy and healthy are those who leave? Is there a sense that in some way or another they're graduating, moving in answer to God's call to new responsibilities, greater fruitfulness and exercise of gifts? Has their service been celebrated and are they sent out with blessing?

On the other extreme, some staff are summarily terminated. They leave like whipped puppies, so wounded that they either take a complete break from all church responsibilities or leave ministry altogether and engage in some other business. If this is the case, it may signal the church's history of relational carnage. I know of a few toxic churches where a sense of dread pervades throughout the ranks of the entire church: with bated breath, one wonders who's next to get torched.

If the internal church family is challenged, I have little expectation that as an outsider I'll have much influence. If there is long list of guest preachers whom the church has hosted "for a season," it may be that as soon as that outsider has brought any critical reflection to bear on the life of the church, they are immediately *persona non grata*.

In all their diversity the New Testament churches reflect the interdependence of local fellowships. It is not just a first century dynamic. I do not know of a healthy church that does not receive regular apostolic oversight. Once recognized, it's obvious. The senior leadership of a local fellowship is not meant to steer through all of the challenges, conflicts and responsibilities on their own. When Paul writes of the church in Ephesians 2:20 he says, *"the members of God's household ... are built on the foundations of the apostles and the prophets."* Because God continues to build His Church, He continues to raise up those who are gifted to bring apostolic oversight.

Similarly, in Ephesians 4:11–13, Paul categorically declares that the Lord, *"has given some to be apostles ... to equip God's people for work in his service, for the building up of the body of Christ, until we all attain to the unity inherent in our faith ... measured by nothing less that the full stature of Christ."* The word "equip" in verse 12 – *katartismon* – means "to perfect, complete, mend, repair, improve, adjust." Because we have not yet attained the unity or the maturity that the Lord purposes for us, we still need those gifted with apostolic authority to help bring us to the fullness that the Lord purposes for us.

As a frustrated Baptist pastor I realized that one of my problems was that while I had denominational executives over me, I did not have anyone exercising any apostolic authority and gifting in either my life or the life of the church. I found it very sobering to have to try to address the lack: if a church does not have apostolic oversight, what foundation is it built on?

A detailed consideration of apostolicity is beyond the mandate of this book. The following sketch is meant only to underscore some of the more dynamic particulars as they apply to the life and health of a local church. Apostolic authority, for instance, needs clarification. It is not determined by how many churches someone has planted and how big those churches have grown. It is not about how many fellowships a person oversees, or the growth strategies and goals they have for their network. Apostolic authority ultimately has one test: *depth of relationship with Jesus.* A church should be able to say of their apostle, "No one we know walks closer to Jesus than he does."

Historically, apostles are first contemplatives. Their time alone with Jesus is the source of their intimacy, their authority, and the timely revelation that they bring. The church is not built on what they've heard on someone else's CDs.

Characteristically, apostles have spent time either in the desert or prison. Often they've frequented both. The maps in the backs of our study bibles ought to mark the apostle Paul's travels to both the churches he worked with and the jails with which he was familiar.

Few apostles in the West have literally spent time in the desert or in prison, but location is not the issue, disposition is. Two issues need discerning: *how much undistracted time have they spent alone with God* and *how much have they suffered?* While the first question has been detailed, the second needs elaboration. In 2 Corinthians 12:12, Paul states that the chief mark of an apostle is longsuffering. The NIV translates the word *hypomone* as *"great perseverance."* The REB uses the phrase *"unfailing endurance."* However it is rendered, it is clearly reflected in Paul's autobiographical disclosures as apostle. Earlier in 2 Corinthians he had written, *"if distress is our lot, it is the price we pay for your consolation and salvation"* (2 Corinthians 1:6). When Paul challenges the authority of the *"super-apostles"* who are attempting to exercise ungodly control and draw the Corinthians away from their *"single-hearted devotion to Christ"* (2 Corinthians 11:3–5), he asks, *"Are they servants of Christ? I am mad to speak like this, but I can outdo them: more often overworked, more often imprisoned, scourged more severely, many a time face to face with death . . ."* (2 Corinthians 11:23). Paul is not bragging perversely. Rather, he is essentially asking of the false apostles, have they been through the refining fire? He himself has been *"disciplined by suffering"* (2 Corinthians 6:9). Has their character been forged by heat and anvil?

An apostle can only exercise true authority when his spirit rules over his soul. Nothing of personal comfort and security ought to compromise the word that the apostle brings. Paul says that he knows what it is to *"abase and abound"* (Philippians 4:12 KJV), *"to have nothing . . . and have plenty."* Because his spirit rules over his soul he is as free to celebrate as he is to sacrifice. That freedom means that the apostle comes to a local church with no personal agenda and zero insistence on personal rights and privileges. He is not governed by feelings, fears or personal needs. In this, true apostolicity is never a hierarchic position of power, but a radically humble service ministry. The church does not exist for the apostles; it is the apostles who exist for the church.

Thus, there are no self-appointed apostles. It is totally inappropriate for someone to show up at house group and announce, "Your apostle is here; now we can get down to business." The Babel bent that seeks to *"make a name for ourselves"* (Genesis 11:4) is a sure sign of bogus motives. And there are no volunteer apostles either. Rather, theirs is an irrefutable commission and authority, as Paul states: *"Through [Christ] I received the privilege of an apostolic commission to bring people of all nations to faith and obedience in his name"* (Romans 1:5). Apostles are sent out by God with trans-local giftings to establish and equip the Church in her life and mission.

One may claim, however, that God has anointed and commissioned them with apostolic authority; who is to say that theirs is a legitimate calling? The biblical witness seems to imply that a man does not realize he is an apostle until others receive him as a timely gift from God and gratefully place themselves under his guidance.

Apostolicity is an intensely relational ministry, one that is exercised from the platform and pulpit, and even more so over dinner, a walk, or in regular conversations on the phone. It may be that time together on the golf course is counted more significant than what occurs over the course of a church weekend!

Personal vulnerability is a characteristic mark of the relationship: Paul says, *"Our affection was so deep that we shared with you not only the gospel but our very selves"* (1 Thessalonians 2:8). So too, is constancy: *"I continually remember you in my prayers"* (Romans 1:9). This remembering could be paraphrased, "Thinking of you and God together." It is the opposite of "out of sight, out of mind."

Another mark of apostolic authority is personal accountability. A general consideration of accountability follows later on in this chapter, and what applies to each of us applies to those with apostolic authority, only more so: *"From everyone who has been given much shall much be required; and to whom they entrusted much, of him they will ask all the more"* (Luke 12:48 NASB). Jesus addressed these concluding words to His disciples when He spoke of leadership within the household of God. As the apostle is to function over the church like a wise and faithful steward managing the master's property, this warning must be taken to heart by anyone attempting to give apostolic oversight.

If a local church is seriously committed to raising up oaks of righteousness they must have answers to these very specific questions: "Who is speaking into our lives? Who brings strong, loving and wise counsel to bear? Who asks the foundational questions, especially of leadership? Who brings a spiritual objectivity and helps to discern what the Spirit is saying to the church? Who helps us appropriate the current dynamics of the larger church worldwide?"

For many churches these questions pose a very practical problem. Just as you can't walk up to someone and ask, "Will you be my friend?" it would be equally inappropriate to walk up to a godly and gifted individual and ask, "Will you be our apostle?" But as this oversight is God's idea, it is also His to provide. In His kindness there is providential truth in the old saying, "When the student is ready, the teacher arrives."

Servant leadership is a very challenging tension. Leading those whom we serve has us walking a tightrope. We can easily fall off on either side. Strong denominational churches often face a different set of problems with regard to corrupt and compromised authority and control issues. I've been with Anglican clergy who describe themselves as "bishop bullied." It's been evident that other pastors are "council compromised." For multiple reasons, these harassed and haggard clergy are unable to give anything much by way of significant leadership.

At a large pastors' conference recently, I asked in passing, "How many of you live a life of fear?" Over ninety percent of the gathered raised their hands. With a few more questions, I narrowed the focus: the most prevalent fear in ministry was that people were going to leave the church. While this fear is more than understandable, it's also a given. People are going to leave. We should count on it.

If the doggerel isn't too calloused, there's great freedom in the truth, "We choose whom we lose." Do we continuously lower the bar so that we don't upset anyone? This can be the excessive and unhealthy pendulum swing of trying to be seeker friendly or culturally sensitive in a pluralistic culture. There are folks presently in church who will not suffer any further compromise. More than likely, those whose hearts are set on the kingdom have already absented themselves. They want to follow a leader who clearly and courageously sees the way forward and enables them to live a faith and a life that has kingdom consequence.

Rather than losing ground, or just barely maintaining the status quo, there are churches that keep raising the bar. These are fellowships that are intentionally contending to see the kingdom of heaven more fully revealed in their midst. Rather than focusing on increasing their numbers, theirs is an ongoing attentiveness to the Lord's present calling. They expect to exercise an ever-increasing commitment as they live out the larger vision that they are given. They recognize that there are folks who cannot or will not rise to the occasion. They understand the feeling that too much is required of them. But rather than complain about the "cost of discipleship" these stalwarts have considered the alternative. I know of one pastor who has Dallas Willard's studied reflections taped to his fridge door:

The cost of nondiscipleship is far greater – even when this life alone is considered – than the price paid to walk with

Jesus. Nondiscipleship costs abiding peace, a life pene-
trated throughout by love, faith that sees everything in the
light of God's overriding governance for good, hope-
fulness that stands firm in the most discouraging of
circumstances, power to do what is right and withstand
the forces of evil. In short, it costs exactly that abundance
of life Jesus said He came to bring.[2]

It's not hard to find a church that expects little more of its
membership than regular attendance and token financial support. It is a rare church that is uncompromised and undistracted
in its kingdom mandate dynamically preaching good news,
healing the sick, bringing peace to the tormented and caring for
the poor.

There are church families that are unwilling to contend for
the kingdom. Recently, I was with a pastor who had become
chronically frustrated. He had served his present church for
many years, but was still at odds with his elders and the church
family over some pretty basic expectations about his job
description. I encouraged him to write his "ministry manifesto"
and submit it to the elders. I suggested that he detail the core
values, mandate and priorities that, by God's grace, he would
not compromise. Upon studied reflection he and the elders
together could decide if he had a future with them. I quoted
Martin Luther's famous declaration in defense of his Ninety-
Five Theses: "Here I stand, I can do no other. God help
me." There comes a moment when time for dithering is long
past.

Along with the spectacular numerical growth of the mega-
churches have been the inglorious scandals perpetrated by
some of the senior leadership. Jimmy Bakker, founder and
former president of PTL, was asked why his autobiography,

---

[2] Dallas Willard, *The Spirit of the Disciplines*, HarperSanFrancisco, 1991, p. 263.

I Was Wrong, written from prison, ran over six hundred pages in length. He answered candidly, "I was that wrong."

Once the tragic news of moral failure is in the public domain, one is left wondering, how could this happen? One of the answers is that these anointed men of God had no one alongside them. They had dozens, maybe even hundreds working for them, but had no one who really knew them or were given permission to speak into their lives. Bakker candidly admitted, "[Those] who tried to warn me to slow me down or to take stock of what I was doing received little appreciation from me."[3]

Just as a healthy church needs apostolic oversight, so every one of us needs a special someone without whom our lives would be shipwrecked. There are times and seasons when we each need to have a trusted friend speak into our lives and ask us the hard questions. If we are to live accountable lives we need to have invited a select few to kick us up the backside when we need it most, and to keep kicking until we get our lives sorted.

In 2000, Nev Green, who was then the worship leader of The Gathering Place in Blandford Forum, Dorset, England began traveling with me on occasion. On our second trip together it became obvious to both of us that the Lord was partnering us in ministry. While we were talking about some of what that might mean, I asked Nev a bald-faced question: "If we're going to be working together I need to know up front – do you have a secret life?" The question took him by surprise, so I bought him some time by saying, "There's been more than enough scandal brought upon the Body of Christ of late. I don't want to play any part in adding to that sorry history." Nev then responded to my question: "I know that you're not asking after sinless perfection. You want to know about integrity and purity of heart. No, I do not have a scandalous secret life."

I knew Nev didn't. I knew of the time he spent alone with

---

[3] Jim Bakker, *I Was Wrong*, Thomas Nelson Publishers, Nashville, 1996, p. 468.

God and I know that you cannot spend significant time alone with God and have a secret life. The light necessarily drives out the darkness. All in, however, it felt important that this kind of transparency should characterize the outset of our ministry together.

Nev and I have become best friends. Part of that friendship is our covenanted submission to one another. Our lives are laid open before one another. We have given each other the formal permission to ask the hardest of questions. We have agreed that there are no questions that we're unwilling to ask and no questions that, once asked, we're unwilling to answer.

I don't have any hesitation or reservation in declaring that I'm accountable to Nev. I have no hesitation or reservation in making myself accountable to him because I don't know anyone else who spends time alone with God like he does. I therefore have the greatest of confidence that what he brings forth will be closer to the heart of God than what I'd get from anyone else, anywhere else.

That having been said, "accountability" needs to be demystified. I need to take personal responsibility for my life. I need to take personal responsibility in submitting myself to Nev and take my concerns to him *before* he has to ask me the hard questions. Otherwise, there's a good chance his confrontation will come ten months too late. It will take that long for Nev to become sufficiently convinced that I'm out of line, that something's definitely not right, that I'm not "myself." By then, I won't just be on the rocks, I will have been shipwrecked.

I know that Nev will be there for me when I call and say, "I need to talk, *now.*"

Because the need for this kind of relational covering is so great, and the image so compelling, it serves to rehearse what I wrote about the tortoise in *Our Eyes Fixed on Jesus*. When Paul admonishes us to put on the armor of God in Ephesians 6:10–18, the entire passage is addressed not to an individual believer, but to the Church. The pronouns are all plural. The whole metaphor is a corporate calling. We will not be able to stand alone.

When we are commended to *"take up the great shield of faith"* the shield Paul names is the *thyreos*, derived from the word *thyra*, meaning "door." A Roman soldier would hold this massive shield in his left hand and the right two-thirds of the shield would cover his left side. The left third of the shield covered his mate's exposed right. When the troops were in position, they created a defensive formation called the "tortoise." When the legionaries held their shields overhead, and the front rows interlocked their shields, they created a kind of shell-like armor that shielded them against missiles both from above and out front.[4]

In these tight ranks, each soldier was dependent on the other for protection. One suddenly understands why there have been so many casualties in the Church, for we have characteristically been far too individualistic, both in our understanding of ministry and spiritual warfare. It is not hard for many of us to think of those who are not only no longer in church, but are no longer walking with the Lord. For a time they fought a valiant fight, but because no one was standing at their side, they were vulnerable targets for the *"burning arrows of the evil one."*[5]

Six months after Nev took over The Gathering Place as senior pastor, I asked him, "How're you doing?" He answered, thoughtfully, "Fine, as long as I keep reminding myself that the job is impossible." It's a great answer for all of us.

If church is to be a supernatural enterprise we ought to rehearse regularly Zechariah 4:6, " *'Not by might nor by power, but by my Spirit,' says the LORD Almighty."*

[4] Kate Gilliver and Michael Whitley, *Rome at War*, Osprey Pub., Oxford, 2005, p. 113.
[5] Ephesians 6:16.

It is impossible to raise up and be raised up as oaks of righteousness in our own strength and gifting. Jesus warned Nicodemus, *"Flesh gives birth to flesh, but the Spirit gives birth to spirit"* (John 3:6 NIV).

Gospel ministry is a fruitfulness that is beyond what is naturally possible and unless we are familiar with New Testament agricultural practices, the conclusion to the parable of the sower may be lost on us. Jesus said that kingdom seed yields thirty, sixty, even a hundredfold harvest (Mark 4:8). The farmers of His day would not have misunderstood His point. Because growing conditions in Palestine were harsh, a ten percent yield would have been considered a plentiful harvest and seven and a half percent an average one.[6]

Jesus announced supernatural, superabundant yield to kingdom ministry, in spite of seemingly insurmountable difficulties and opposition – thieving spirits, barren ground and worldly compromise (Mark 4:15–19). His warning to the Sadducees ought to give us pause: *"Do ye not therefore err, because ye know not . . . the power of God"* (Mark 12:24 KJV).

Are we living out of a supernatural calling or not?

---

[6] Joachim Jeremias, *The Parables of Jesus*, SCM Press, London, 1972, fn. 86, p. 150.

3

Church Atmosphere

In September 2003 I was invited to preach a tour of several churches in the Ukraine. When I arrived in Kiev my host asked if there was anything particular I wanted to see while we were in the capital city. I had done a little web research prior to my arrival and so I surprised him with the specificity of my request: "Could we go to the Gate Church of the Trinity?" As it was only half an hour away from the airport, my host graciously accommodated my request.

The Gate Church was built in 1106 and is the entrance to the Monastery of the Caves. The outside of the church is covered with nine large frescoes. Each one is a larger than life depiction of the holy men who founded and sustained the monastery. As it was mid-afternoon by the time we got there, the golden orbs that surround the saints' heads dazzled in the bright autumn sunshine.

On entering the church it was the aroma that was arresting. The inside of the church is permeated with incense, just as the sanctuary has been saturated with the prayers of the faithful over the centuries. Breathing deeply, I was filled with a wonderfully rich and compelling peace, grace and light.

Few church buildings are such a sensory feast of sight and smell. But every church has its own atmosphere, one that is created by the people that gather there. Every church has a spiritual thermostat. Some are set such that church is cold, even frosty, and feels almost like a hostile environment. Some seem compelled to conserve precious resources and consequently feel empty, vacuous and marginally able to support life. Others feel safe, hospitable and generously welcoming.

The physical ambiance of the building is a minor determinant. The lighting, the colors of paint and carpet, the arrangement and style of seating each contribute in small ways to the spiritual temperature of a church. But the overall climate of the place is predominantly determined by the gathered. It's easiest to get a reading on a particular church at the opening and close of a given service. In some places, people come in, sit down, and are remiss to even make eye contact with one another – unless it's to scowl at a visitor and then the message is unmistakable: "You don't belong here. If you did, you'd know that you were sitting in my seat." Once the benediction is pronounced, everyone takes off like scared jackrabbits. In other fellowships, true to their nature, there is a genuine welcome and engagement, especially of the newcomer. At the close of the service, folks are slow to leave both the presence of God and one another.

One end of the continuum is an assembly of strangers at best, antagonists at worst; the other end is a gathering of friends, new and old, where one's glad to belong.

Love is the hallmark of the healthiest of churches. It has always been so. At the close of the second century, the Roman Emperor and military dictator Septimus Severus passed a universal decree that outlawed, on pain of death, conversion to either Christianity or Judaism. It was an edict that was ruthlessly enforced as the Church father Clement of Alexandria testified: "Many martyrs are daily burned, confined, or beheaded, before our eyes." Another father, Tertullian, attempted to bring redress to the persecution in a brilliant philosophical appeal that called for the freedom of religion. (Among the many allegations of the time, believers were falsely accused of sacrificing infants during the celebration of the Lord's Supper and of promoting incest.) In his *Apology,* written around AD 200, Tertullian delineated what he called "the peculiarities of Christian society" and contrasted the lives of the believers with those of the pagan state. He says of the former, "We are a body knit together as such by a common religious profession, by unity of discipline, and by the bond of a common hope." As to the accusations that have been brought against Christians he says,

> But it is mainly the deeds of a love so noble that lead many to put a brand upon us. *See,* they say, *how they love one another,* for they themselves are animated by mutual hatred; how they are ready even to die for one another, for they themselves will sooner put to death. And they are wroth with us, too, because we call each other brethren; for no other reason, as I think, than because among themselves names of consanguinity are assumed in mere pretence of affection. But we are your brethren as well, by the law of our common mother nature, though you are hardly men, because brothers so unkind. At the same time, how much more fittingly they are called and counted brothers who have been led to the knowledge of God as their common Father, who have drunk in one spirit of holiness, who from the same womb of a common ignorance have agonized into the same light of truth! But on this very account, perhaps, we are regarded as having less claim to be held true brothers, that no tragedy makes a noise about our brotherhood, or that the family possessions, which generally destroy brotherhood among you, create fraternal bonds among us. One in mind and soul, we do not hesitate to share our earthly goods with one another. All things are common among us but our wives.[1]

It is not particularly difficult to "create fraternal bonds." Love is simple. One of the characteristics of the apostle Paul's

[1] Tertullian, *Apology,* 39.7, *Ante-Nicene Fathers,* vol. 3, Hendrickson Pub. Co., Peabody, Mass., 1994, p. 46.

letters is his gratitude. He usually declares it openly within the first few verses: *"I thank my God every time I think of you."* [2]

One church I work with forms what they call a "circle of blessing." On occasion, they take turns going round the circle, declaring their appreciation of one another. One after another they explicitly honor someone in the fellowship. Every church could improve its atmosphere by celebrating a similar circle of blessing, even if a measure of creative liberty is required. When it's the church grump's turn in the circle, one can always say to him, "I really appreciate those rare occasions when you smile. It means a lot to me."

Just as some individuals have great difficulty saying the words, "I love you," some churches are similarly challenged when it comes to declaring their appreciation.

As I spend time with local churches, it is often very evident that those on staff are worn out and fed up. It's not uncommon for associates or elders to confide that their senior pastor very rarely thanks them for their hard work and dedicated service.

When praise is rare and encouragement is infrequent, it is a sure sign of an unhealthy environment. When there are very few celebrations, it usually signals that people are operating in survival mode and that characteristically makes for a chilly church climate. Like the sign that gets posted at a golf course on occasion, some morning's worship ought to be postponed because of frost delay.

Spiritual hypothermia takes a deadly toll. I have spent many long evenings listening to the distress of those who, for all manner of reasons, have allowed themselves to be squeezed into roles that require well-armored personas to survive. But living a false self necessarily means that we have forfeited our true identity. Chronic discontent, depression and burnout signal a diseased, and dis-eased, spirit.

[2] Philippians 1:6. See also Romans 1:8, 1 Corinthians 1:4, Ephesians 1:16, Colossians 1:3, 1 Thessalonians 1:2, 2 Thessalonians 1:3, 2 Timothy 1:3 and Philemon 1:4.

We can only grow towards health, happiness and holiness if we are true to ourselves and real with one another.

But what is "real?"

I can offer no better explanation than to quote from the magnificent children's classic, *The Velveteen Rabbit*. What follows is the conversation between a newly arrived stuffed Rabbit and the patriarch of the nursery toys, the Skin Horse.

"What is REAL?" asked the Rabbit one day . . .

"Real isn't how you are made," said the Skin Horse. "It's a thing that happens to you . . . "

"Does it hurt?" asked the Rabbit.

"Sometimes," said the Skin Horse, for he was always truthful. "When you are Real you don't mind being hurt."

"Does it happen all at once, like being wound up, or bit by bit?"

"It doesn't happen all at once," said the Skin Horse. "You become. It takes a long time. That's why it doesn't happen often to people who break easily, or have sharp edges, or who have to be carefully kept. Generally, by the time you are Real, most of your hair has been loved off, and your eyes drop out and you get loose in the joints and very shabby. But these things don't matter at all, because once you are Real you can't be ugly, except to people who don't understand." [3]

✤ ✤ ✤

We can't have fun together if we're not real with one another. Healthy laughter and true enjoyment of one another are grounded in integrity and purity of heart, rooted in openness and honesty. And *Reader's Digest* is right: laughter is the best medicine.

Years ago when our attempts at planting a church were met with insurmountable challenges, my associate, Kim, took me

[3] Margery Williams, *The Velveteen Rabbit*, Ariel Books, Kansas City, 1991, p. 10.

slot car racing. I have absolutely no interest in slot cars. He's a NASCAR guy; I dutifully spent the hour with him, knowing that this was his "thing." On our way back to the church office, I asked him why he was so keen to take me with him. He grinned and said, "You needed to crash something and have it not matter." The tears were soon redemptively rolling down our cheeks.

Improving church atmosphere is not difficult. Eddie Mason is the pastor of Southside Christian Fellowship in McDonough, Georgia. He is one of the most loving men I've ever met. You can't get anywhere near him without him saying, "Let me hug on your neck." Not surprisingly the church, following his lead, is a very warm and caring fellowship. Their church phone message not only rehearses part of their mission statement, it *is* who they are: "Welcome to Southside Christian Fellowship. In this place you are loved, accepted and received."

Eddie told me the following story.

"My daughter-in-law, Tamie, wanted her brother to come to church, but he just wasn't very interested in doing the 'church thing.' He was having some problems in his personal life and both Tamie and Sherry, their mother, continued to encourage him to 'get right with God.' He decided that the only way he was going to shut them up was to dutifully go to church.

Sunday came and, true to his word, he showed up at church. He was wearing combat boots, cut-off jeans and a ragged tee shirt, intentionally showing off the colorful tattoos that covered his arms. He wore his best earrings and nose ring and expected to be met with disdain and judgment. To his surprise he was accepted and received. He was so overcome by the love he experienced, he committed his life to the Lord at the end of the service. To this day he loves the Lord and the church."

As we're all varying degrees of personality types, some of us are definitely not huggie types. How then do we love on people? We each have to find a way, for there is tremendous truth in the doggerel, "People don't care how much you know until they know how much you care."

In this regard there is a remarkable passage of scripture in Deuteronomy 14 on the tithe, one that is rarely taught. It is a wonderful declaration of the Lord's openhandedness and His love of celebration. In essence, it's a call to party: *"Feast with rejoicing, you and your family, in the presence of the* LORD *your God"* (Deuteronomy 14:26c).

If we understand that God is our Father, then we should also know that we have a larger family than we're presently living with. If we eat together in His presence and extend our relational circle, we intentionally make our family bigger. Gourmet meals are not required. Church climate improves even when we have coffee with someone we don't yet know. It is one simple way to show that we care.

Again, love is the hallmark of the healthiest churches. How specifically can we answer the question, *"Are we a more loving church now than we were a year ago?"* One significant part of the answer is found on the margins of the church family. Do the newcomers, the recently divorced, the recovering addict, the adult single and the physically and socially challenged feel like they are included? Do they feel like they belong? Are they now counted as friends? Or after two months have they disappeared without anyone noticing?

If numbers are diminishing, it's typically an irrefutable sign that the church suffers a cold, harsh atmosphere. If people are leaving hurt, lonely and disconnected, any talk of "Gideon's radical remnant"[4] is rubbish. People are not leaving because they aren't committed enough. Rather, the lack of love in the "fellowship" makes belonging impossible.

---

[4] In Judges 7:2 and 4 the Lord told Gideon to reduce his army in size from 22,000 to 10,000, and then to a remnant of 300.

When church is understood as the gathering of the friends of God – for those who do not yet have a friend – we are living out the "one another" callings. Throughout the New Testament, relational commitment and engagement receives comprehensive treatment. *"Love one another ... Encourage one another and build each other up ... Belong to one another ... Accept one another ... Honor one another ... Live in agreement with one another ... Pray for one another ... Admonish one another ... Have mutual concern for one another ... Carry one another's burdens ... Forgive one another ... Serve one another in love ... Spur one another on toward love and good deeds."* [5]

In his book, *Shaped by God's Heart*, Milfred Minatrea suggests a most evocative exercise to test the health of the local church. [6] The "one another" scriptures are written on 3 × 5 inch recipe cards. The cards are passed round to the members of a small group and everyone takes a turn placing his or her card on a table, arranging or rearranging the different cards on a scale of one to ten. The discussion that ensues helps discern which "one another" the church is best – and worst – at. If everyone agrees that the church is not brilliant on any front, it's time to *"confess your sins to one another"* (James 5:16) and recognize that when the majority of the gathered go home from church feeling lonelier and more desperate than when they came in, it's a pseudo-community, not a church family.

In contrast, I know of a church that would have done very well in this exercise. They were a racially intermixed fellowship of whites, blacks and Hispanics. What really set the church apart was their inclusion of the group with alternative hair color. It was mostly electric green. I preached almost a week of meetings there and each night when I gave the invitation, their leader, a young man with a stunning blue Mohawk, brought

[5] John 13:34; 1 Thessalonians 5:11; Romans 12:6; Romans 15:7; Romans 12:10, NIV; Romans 12:16; James 5:16; Colossians 3:16, NIV, 1 Corinthians 12:25, NET; Galatians 6:2; Colossians 3:13, NIV; Galatians 5:13; Hebrews 10:24, NIV.

[6] Milfred Minatrea, *Shaped by God's Heart*, Jossey-Bass, San Francisco, 2004, p. 50.

several of the green-hairs forward and we prayed together as they gave their lives to the Lord. Later in the evening, several young women with chopped and bleached hair, black makeup and face piercings came forward for prayer.

One night after the service, the pastor's wife was evidently challenged by the church's unconditional inclusion. She took me aside and exclaimed, "You know those girls we prayed for together – they're *lesbians*!!" That I knew. I tried to refocus the conversation. "Isn't it wonderful that they felt accepted enough to come to church and receive something of the love of God?"

The healthiest churches understand that their mandate is to welcome, heal, pardon and save – and leave judgment to our gracious and merciful God.

What sets the spiritual temperature of a local church more than anything else is the place they make for the poor. We typically think in economic terms when we think of the poor – the hungry, the homeless, the destitute. Biblically, the term is more comprehensive – the poor are the *powerless* – those who are overwhelmed by life's problems. This kind of poverty is far more comprehensive than sheer economics. A healthy church finds ways to serve the powerless; a really healthy church some- how finds ways of living *with* the powerless.

To my horror and not-so-righteous indignation, I was recently shown a church leadership newsletter. In it was the following statement: "Great leaders get rid of 'problem people,' and replace them with 'solution people.'" I looked at my friend, who had shown me the article, and asked, "Has this guy ever read the gospels? Would he describe the first disciples as 'solution people'? The only 'solution guy' on the team was Judas!"

If indeed we read the Good Book and live even a bit of life, we have to conclude that "all God's children got problems."

One way or another, we are all a sandwich short of a picnic. If a "great leader" gets rid of all the problem people, things are more like the TV series *Survivor* than church, only without immunity. There will be no one left. In fact, if he's ruthlessly honest this "great leader" will have to vote himself off the island.

Healthy churches have home groups in one form or another, for it's there, face-to-face, week in and week out, that the essence of true church life is thrashed out. That said, the small group is an inspiring concept, but a brutal reality. I once attended a cell church conference and at one point the instructor put up an overhead of a large circle that represented the small group. Inside the circle there was an L, the leader. There was an AL for the apprentice leader and an H for the host. Then there were seven or eight little stick men and women for the others in the group. Off in the corner was an EGR. While all the other initials were self-evident, none of us knew what an EGR was.

The explanation was forthcoming. Five weeks into a small group's life everybody absolutely knows who the EGR is. No matter what the discussion, it's always about them. They dominate every single meeting. Their need for attention is boundless. The instructor said, "The EGR is the one that makes you want to jump off the couch, dash across the room, put your hands around his or her neck and throttle them while saying, 'I'm sorry, but I have to kill you now.'" (I recently told this story during the course of a teaching time and someone shouted out, "Are we allowed to do that?")

The initials EGR stand for Extra Grace Required. Given that grace is to be *"multiplied"* to each of us (2 Peter 1:2 NASB), we are all EGRs. With utmost sincerity, we ought to gather in our small groups every week, hold hands and say out loud to one another, "Please be nice to me, I'm an EGR."

Such an atmosphere of patient and loving acceptance contributes tremendously to church health. I was recently with a church who serve a pancake breakfast every Sunday morning. They typically prepare over one hundred and fifty plates for the local street people and the marginalized, EGRs every one of them. I spoke at length with one of the greeters whose job it was to seat and socialize with those who came to be fed. As he told me story after story, it was evident that those enjoying the breakfast were otherwise overwhelmed by life's problems. But there in the church basement, for at least one morning a week, they knew that they belonged, that they were loved, and that they were listened to.

"Life is difficult." That telling sentence is the opening to Scott Peck's bestselling book, *The Road Less Traveled*. Life is difficult for all of us and that's why we all need extra grace. What we do in the face of hardship and how we appropriate the Lord's grace is what makes us who we are. The challenges we face forge both our character and our personality, and determine the nature and course of whatever ministry we're involved in.

These truths were underscored over the course of a weekend with a church that was not very healthy at all. It would have been miraculous for it to have been otherwise, as the senior leader was one of the most cynical, negative and faultfinding individuals I have ever worked with. As some of the details of his life unfolded, there was no question that he'd faced a great deal of disappointment, heartache and grief. There was also no question that it had exacted a tremendous toll.

This man actually looked so much like a sour puss, I thought of an exchange between Abraham Lincoln and his aide. Lincoln commented, "I don't like the looks of that man's face." The shocked aide responded, "Mr. President, you can't hold a man responsible for his looks." Lincoln answered, "Any man over forty is responsible for the way his face looks." The playwright and poet Oscar Wilde felt it took a little longer, stating, "By the age of 50 you have the face you deserve."

By middle age, a man's habitual responses to life's hardships are so well established they literally etch themselves on his face. A woman's too. We're tight-lipped or sullen, we're frowners, or sulkers, or pouters; we furrow our brows such that they're indelibly creased; if pensive by nature, we will squint slightly. Alternatively, there may be a characteristic little grin that keeps the corners of our mouths lifted and our eyes bright and open; truly happy people literally have a brightness about them.

By the time we're forty our life choices are characteristically consistent. We're each pretty settled when it comes to seeing the proverbial glass half full or half empty. It shows on our face, somewhat like car tires. After 80,000 kilometers the wear bars start showing and any alignment problems are visibly obvious.

I learned this twenty years ago when I attended a leadership conference where we worked through an exercise that profoundly changed my life. We were asked to think of the person we most respected, honored or admired. We were then asked to name the single quality that makes them the person they are. Twenty qualities were soon listed on the whiteboard before us.

Because the exercise had such a lasting effect on me, I sometimes use it during the course of a church weekend. This was the list of qualities that was generated the last time I worked the exercise: the people that were most respected, honored and admired were: peaceful, faithful, humble, gentle, consistent, wise, loving, fun-loving, humorous. They had high integrity. They were courageous, accepting, bold, patient, discerning, generous, attentive listeners, holy, carefree, childlike.

Each of those qualities is either a skill or an attitude; a few are a combination of the two. A skill is a learned ability. An attitude is a choice. The first has us drawing from past experience, the second from present grace. To make the point, suppose being a good golfer was what we most admired. Golf is a skill. It requires hours and hours of practice. One can only be a good golfer after hitting thousands and thousands of balls, and playing hundreds of rounds. One can't simply choose to be a great golfer, though a bad attitude will never improve one's score.

By way of contrast, integrity is a choice. In a given situation we choose right or wrong. When faced with compromise we choose either righteousness or complicity. And while character is formed through a series of consistent choices, we have the opportunity to make new choices in each and every situation. We may have a long history of lying. In a given instance we could choose to tell the truth and face the consequences.

The vast majority of the qualities we most respect, honor and admire are attitudes. Typically, around 80% of the character-istics that get named are attitudes. In the list above, being peaceful, faithful, humble, gentle, consistent, accepting, bold, patient, courageous, generous, carefree and childlike are all attitudes. Being humorous is an exception. It's a skill. Among other things, it requires a sense of timing. There are some people who just cannot tell a joke, even though they want to be funny.

I continue to be both confounded and inspired by the facts that (1) we choose our attitudes, (2) those choices deter-mine our character, and (3) our attitudinal choices profoundly effect our relationships. I am confounded because I know that I can be having a growl with one of my kids, yet answer the phone politely, engage in civil and respectful conversation, then hang up the phone and immediately start growling at my child again. How does that happen? I choose to let loose my frustration; I rein in my aggravation and choose to be calm, convivial and a good listener on the phone, and then I choose to lose it again, consciously forfeiting the present grace available to communicate respectfully with my child.

Most of the time we have little control over what happens to us. We do, however, decide what happens in us. This is very evident in airports. A few years ago I was patiently awaiting my boarding announcement when we were suddenly told that because of mechanical difficulties, the flight had been canceled. Knowing the drill, those of us who were frequent flyers immediately jumped out of our seats and ran back to the check-in counter to try to make alternative travel arrangements.

The man in line ahead of me was an irate, vulgar man. I had no difficulty overhearing as he ripped into the ticket agent: *"This ******* airline has to get me home for Yom Kippur."* A long string of insulting profanity followed. (Yom Kippur is the Jewish Day of Atonement, the last day of the solemn ten-day fast.) He continued to rant and rave while the agent tried to find him a flight, but apologized that there were no more direct flights until the next day. Before she could offer any alternatives, he swore at her again and stormed off to book a flight with another airline.

By the time I was standing in front of her, the ticket agent was nearly in tears. Her hands were visibly shaking. In an effort to try to help her through her upset, I smiled and said, "Hi. I'm not the guy that was just here. Take a cleansing breath. That guy was not nice. I'm nice." I smiled again. "When can you get me back to Toronto?" She blinked, collected herself, smiled weakly and began hunting for a flight. Moments later she said, "If you're willing to run, I can get you on the flight to Vancouver, and then Vancouver to Toronto, and you'll get home just over two hours later than you would have on the direct flight."

Both the guy ahead of me and I faced exactly the same set of circumstances, ones which were beyond our control. The two of us chose very different attitudes – and got very different responses. John Milton, in his classic *Paradise Lost*, put the matter precisely: "The mind is its own place, And in itself/ Can make a heav'n of hell, a hell of heav'n."[7]

I love to learn. I count myself a lifelong student and will continue to learn new things as long as my brain functions. That being said, it still astounds me that what really makes a

---

[7] John Milton, *Paradise Lost*, Bk. 1.254–5, Odyssey Press, Indianapolis, 1976, p. 13.

difference in my life, and what determines the influence I have over those around me, I choose.

Our individual attitudes cumulatively determine church atmosphere. In 1 Corinthians 12 Paul teaches on the gifts of the Spirit at work in a local church and asserts that together we make up the Body of Christ. Each member is an indispensable part of the whole and the interdependence is to be such that we not only work together but that as a body, *"all its parts might feel the same concern for one another. If one part suffers, all suffer together; if one flourishes, all rejoice together"* (1 Corinthians 12:25–26). Together as a body, our corporate attitude creates the church's climate. If a local church's attitudinal aggregate is taken, which outweighs the other: encouragement, gratitude and hopeful expectation, or criticism, faultfinding and judgmentalism? Moses's words regarding Israel's prosperity and wellbeing are appropriately applied to the local church: *"I offer you the choice of life or death, blessing or curse. Choose life and you and your descendants will live"* (Deuteronomy 30:19). The attitudinal choices we make have consequences for those with whom we live, let alone the generation that follows.

Life is difficult, but love is simple. During a weekend church conference I stayed locally with very good friends who were not part of the host church family. Lamentably, my friends weren't worshiping anywhere at the time, for they were in recovery. They had been very devoted and committed members in a church that had become toxic, if not abusive. One of the many things that had taken a desperate toll was that there was very little gratitude expressed on the part of senior leadership. The pyramid was very definitely point up, and the membership was expected to serve the vision that God had given the senior leader.

A few days after the weekend, the host pastor and his wife dropped in on my friends with a card and a bottle of wine to say "thank you" for putting me up. My friends emailed me to say, "We were hugely touched by that simple act."

4

Generosity

The healthiest, happiest and holiest churches are "lavishly open-handed." That's how the apostle Paul described the churches in Macedonia: *"from the depths of their poverty, they showed themselves lavishly open-handed"* (2 Corinthians 8:2). Philippi was the largest church in Macedonia. As far as our New Testament reads it was, by all accounts, the healthiest, happiest, holiest church Paul worked with, for the Letter to the Philippians is the only epistle he writes without bringing any correction to bear.

Open-handedness is a timeless quality. In all of my travels, I have never met a healthy church that was stingy or an unhealthy church that was generous.

Some church leaders, however, are too intimidated to talk and to teach about money. It's easily discerned by the way they take an offering. Some are evidently embarrassed and under the guise of being "seeker sensitive," they excuse the visitor and the newcomer from the mundane and obligatory duties of the membership. Others are apologetic. Almost nothing is said when it's time for the offering, because, "We don't talk about money here. We trust God." In the extreme, there's a super-spiritual pride in their *weakly* offerings.

This unfounded reticence is unquestionably less than a biblical understanding, for the Scriptures have a great deal to say about money. There is significantly more explicit instruction on money, finances and stewardship in the New Testament than there is on prayer, petition and intercession.

It would be incongruous to boast, "We don't talk about prayer here. We trust God." If indeed the Scriptures are the full and final authority in all matters of faith and conduct, of course we trust God, but we're going to speak about the things that He speaks about.

The gospels give ample evidence that Jesus was not afraid to talk about money. While He tells only two parables about prayer, thirteen of the forty-one parables – roughly one third – have to do with finance. Any church that withholds this revelation of the heart of God deprives its people of that which would wonderfully enrich life, ministry and mission.

The fundamental source of the embarrassment to talk about money is the unwillingness or the inability to contend with idolatry. The decisions we make about our finances are the ultimate bottom line that determine where and in what we find our security, significance and our satisfaction.

Further, the way we spend money is a function of worship. What do we want "more" of? More toys, or more of *"the breadth and length and height and depth of Christ's love"* (Ephesians 4:18–19)? What "more" would increase our sense of security? A larger bank balance and a flusher investment portfolio, or *"the peace of God which is beyond all understanding"* (Philippians 4:7)? What "more" would increase our sense of significance and our satisfaction? A larger house and a faster car, or a greater understanding of our position in Christ and a greater kingdom authority and anointing?

One of the most distinguished of the early Church fathers, Origen of Alexandria, addressed these very same issues over 1,750 years ago:

> Let each one of us now examine himself and silently in his own heart decide which is the flame of love that chiefly and above all else is afire within him . . . Whatever it is that weighs the heaviest in the balance of your affection, that for you is God. But I fear that with very many the

love of gold will turn the scale, that down will come the
weight of covetousness lying heavy in the balance.[1]

If we underline our Bibles, we might do a quick check: is
Matthew 6:24 highlighted? It's a clear description of kingdom
life as Jesus reveals it: *"You cannot serve God and Money."*
Both the REB and the NIV appropriately capitalize the word
Money; the translation of the Greek *mammon*, for money, can
take on the attributes of deity.

It is more than ironic that the words, "In God we trust" are
printed on US currency. When so much of life is spent on what,
for so many, is appropriately called "the pursuit of the Almighty
Dollar," the god trusted in is enshrined in First National Savings
and Loan.

Mammon, however, is not a god of comfort, for it is a god
that is never satisfied. There is never enough. No matter how
much one has, Mammon says there needs to be just a little bit
more. That distorting fear – that there is never enough – is a
greater driving force than greed.

Tight-fisted fear rules and ruins life. It keeps a person's life
small. There is little by way of a legacy of consequence. A huge
financial fortune may be bequeathed, but the stingy have little
else of lasting significance that counts as their heritage. To die
alone, estranged from those who were once one's loved ones,
cannot be considered successful living, irrespective of the
fortune one has generated. King Solomon, the richest man of
his time,[2] markedly contrasts godly values: *"One may give freely
and yet grow richer; another is tight-fisted, yet ends in poverty. A
generous person enjoys prosperity; and one who refreshes others will
be refreshed"* (Proverbs 11:24).

At the other end of the economic spectrum, Jesus was so
poor He had *"nowhere to lay his head"* (Matthew 8:20), yet He

---

[1] Origen, "Homily on the Book of Judges" 2.3, in R.B. Tollington, *Selections from the Commentaries and Homilies of Origen*, London, 1929, pp. 257–258.

[2] 1 Kings 10:23.

was the most generous person who ever lived and it is impossible to overstate His eternal legacy. He directly addresses Mammon's lie of insufficiency when He says, *"Do not be anxious for your life"* (Mathew 6:25 NASB). He directly counters economic idolatry: *"Life is more than food, the body more than clothes ... Can anxious thought add a single day to your life?"* (Matthew 6:25, 27). Jesus explicitly recognizes that the fear of insufficiency drives the heathen, but they don't know who loves them. Not so for the disciple. Jesus assures His followers, *"your heavenly Father knows ... "* He not only knows our needs, but He is the most faithful of providers. For that reason we, as His beloved children, can rest in the knowledge of His generous care and be free to, *"seek first the kingdom of God and his righteousness"* (Matthew 6:33 NIV).

If we, as Christ's Church, are serious about living life as men and women who earnestly desire to see God's will done on earth as in heaven, any question about money gets asked through this lens: "What is God's will for me and my job?" *"Seek first his kingdom ... "* When we're thinking about moving and buying a new house, our first priority is to *"seek first his kingdom ... "* When it's time to buy a new car, we're to *"seek first his kingdom ... "* Investments? *"Seek first his kingdom ... "* Pension contributions? *"Seek first his kingdom ... "* New golf clubs? *"Seek first his kingdom ... "*

Most of us haven't a clue what any of that would mean.

This much is certain: foundational to an understanding of kingdom finances is a healthy understanding of the tithe. As with any foundation, the surer it is established, the greater the building that can be erected. Spiritually, once a healthy understanding of the tithe is established there is tremendous grounding secured and freedom released, and that has tremendous consequence for the life and health of a local church.

The principle of tithing is not so much a function of obedience – because the Bible says we have to – as it is relationship – because we know who we are, and whose we are.

Tithing is the fundamental recognition that all of life and all we have is a gift from God.

The Book of Leviticus has three controlling themes: the purification, holiness and redemption of the people who are called by God. While many readers lose their way in all the detailed rules and regulations, the conclusion to the Book is a clear and timeless truth regardless of culture or context: *"A tithe of everything ... belongs to the* LORD; *it is holy to the* LORD" (Leviticus 27:30 NIV). The Hebrew word *maasar*, translated as "tithe" means simply, "a tenth." A tenth of all that we have belongs to the Lord. It is "holy" – meaning that it is consecrated, set apart, set aside.

While this instruction was given to an agrarian people who were living off the land thousands of years ago, the tithe is a spiritual principle that is applicable regardless how we make our living. The tithe is the fundamental recognition that though we work hard for what we have, it ultimately is not ours. It is not our strength, our ability or our diligence that yields. Whatever strength, ability and diligence we can muster is a gift from God. As King David declared in his praise offering, *"Wealth and honour come from you; you rule over all ... Everything comes from you, and it is only of your gifts that we give to you"* (1 Chronicles 29:12, 14).

It is to be established in our hearts – we are not self-made men and women. That's why we are to, *"honor the* LORD *with* [our] *wealth, with the first-fruits of* [our] *produce"* (Proverbs 3:9). Setting aside ten percent of our gross income, before the taxman gets his claws into it, is the ongoing recognition that all of life is a gift from God.

So that this is firmly established on the surest of ground, let it be settled that the tithe is not just an Old Testament principle. In several places in the gospels Jesus presumes the tithe, and in Romans 11:16 Paul uses the phrase "first fruits," one of the biblical idioms for the tithe, as an illustration. He does so in a way that presumes such an understanding of tithing within the church fellowship that he can take a great deal for granted and even mix his metaphors. *"If . . . the first fruits [are] holy, then the whole batch is holy."* This statement is issued in the context of the apostle's instruction on the place that the Gentiles have in the redemptive purposes of God. In the midst of such lofty doctrines of election and irresistible grace, he uses first fruits, the tithe, to demonstrate that the consecrated portion has determinative consequence on the remaining lump.

What we do with the tithe determines what God does with the rest. The tithe is a test, not just of our gratitude and our self-understanding; it is a test of our faith. Do we believe that God can do more with 90% than we can with 100%? Do we have faith in the Lord's supernatural provision, or is our trust in Mammon, our bank balance? The call to tithe essentially says, "Put your money where your mouth is."

The tithe is also a test of our faithfulness. While the parable of the double-ledgering steward as a whole is a challenging one to interpret,[3] the conclusion is a clear call to financial faithfulness: *"Anyone who can be trusted in small matters can be trusted also in great; and anyone who is dishonest in small matters is dishonest also in great. If, then, you have not proved trustworthy with the wealth of this world, who will trust you with the wealth that is real?"* (Luke 16:10–11). In its context, these kingdom principles override what on face value seems to be praise for the conniving and desperate steward who scrambles to save his skin. Just like the prodigal son in the parable of the Father's love, he too had been squandering his existence. While the prodigal was a wastrel, the steward was set on the ruthless creation of his own private fortune, yet had mismanaged his life and finances with consequences as disastrous as the prodigal's.

---

[3] Archbishop Trench stated, "No one, who has seriously considered, will underrate the difficulties of this parable." *Notes on the Parables*, Macmillan and Co., London, 1877, p. 427. T.W. Manson commented: "This parable has always presented difficulties for the interpreter, and like most of such difficulties they arise from trying to press the details of the story instead of seeking for the main point." *The Mission and Message of Jesus*, Macmillan, 1940, p. 583.

Jesus told the parable of the prodigal son to the scribes and Pharisees to explain why He was the friend of sinners. He addressed the parable of the unjust steward to His disciples to warn them of the consequences of mismanaging their lives and livelihoods.

Elsewhere in the gospels, Jesus contrasts *"treasure on earth,"* money in one form or another, and *"treasure in heaven."*[4] His words to the rich young ruler, for example, imply that heavenly treasure is deposited when the wealth of this world is freely and extravagantly given to the poor.[5] But the conclusion to the parable of the unjust steward is a contrast of yet another commodity.

The prophet Malachi warns that when we withhold the tithe, we *"rob God"* (Malachi 3:8 NIV). Such thieving must be understood rhetorically, as the following verse makes clear: *"You are under a curse – the whole nation of you – because you are robbing me"* (Malachi 3:9).

If we are not faithful with money, we cannot be trusted with the power and authority to heal the sick, release the tormented and preach Good News. That's why the land is cursed – we're not healthy enough to bear such a gift that would bring blessing. When we withhold the tithe, we also squander the redemptive authority that had been entrusted to us. This always has far-reaching consequences.

As a young pastor, I took over an established church whose leadership had not been discipled. Among other things, these kingdom principles of finance had evidently not been modeled, taught or appropriated. It wasn't long before I realized that I had to confront the church treasurer. I called him into my office, spoke about the sorry state of the church's finances and asked him if he tithed. He looked at me with a fierce scowl and retorted, "That's none of your damn business." I thought that was a particularly telling reaction. I calmly replied,

4   Matthew 6:19.
5   Luke 18:22.

"Actually, it's precisely my business. As treasurer, you're one of our spiritual leaders. I need to know if you personally can trust God for the provision of your household, because if you can't do that, then I can't really expect you as treasurer to trust God for the provision of the church household. I'll do everything I can to help you get to that place of trust and freedom. If not, I'll be needing your resignation." With a few more choice words, he resigned there and then.

Any significant position of leadership – pastors, elders, treasurers, worship leaders, prayer ministry team, home group leaders, Sunday School teachers – if not faithful with money cannot be trusted with real wealth. We cannot give significant spiritual leadership if trust in God's supernatural provision isn't settled in our hearts. The eternal consequences of squandering kingdom authority to heal the sick, free the tormented and preach salvation to the lost are far greater than mismanaging earthly wealth.

It is therefore a sad fact that when it comes to finances, the Church in the West is generally not in good shape. Some telling statistics follow. The Canadian Center for Philanthropy surveyed giving patterns in 2004. On average, the regular church attendee gave $395 annually.[6] If they were in church every Sunday of the year, their average offering would amount to $7.60 per week.

Giving in the UK is marginally higher. John Preston, the National Stewardship and Resources Officer for the Church of England proudly declared, "Average weekly giving by Church of England parishioners hit the £5 mark for the first time in 2004 ... Achieving £5 a week is quite a milestone."[7] (At the present rate of exchange, £5 is the equivalent of $10.80 CDN, or $10.27 USD.)

---

[6] "Caring Canadians, Involved Canadians: Highlights from the 2004 Canada Survey"; www.statscan.ca, #71–542–XIE, p. 16.

[7] www.cofe.anglican.org/news/pr9006.html.

To put those numbers in some sort of context, the Canadian Council of Welfare reported that in the same year, 2004, a single parent with one dependent child received a national average welfare payment of $15,600 annually.[8] If that single parent faithfully tithed, his or her weekly offering would be $30.

If every Canadian churchgoer suddenly lost their jobs, went on welfare, but tithed their support checks, giving in the nation's churches would increase nearly *four times*.

Statistics are tricky to interpret. Big numbers can easily skew the results. That is not the case when it comes to charitable giving. Canadian donors with annual incomes of less than $20,000 gave away an average of 1.7% of their pre-tax income. Those with income in excess of $100,000 contributed 0.5% of their pre-tax income.[9]

We in the West wonder why we don't see many kingdom miracles, yet we can't be trusted with what's in our wallets and bank accounts.

While working on this chapter I read a clever headline in *The Guardian*: "Britons' personal debt exceeds Britain's GDP."[10] Given the crushing debt load that so many labor under, the response, "I can't afford to give God 10%" is understandable. It is, however, an unwise and ill-informed one. It is especially those in desperate debt who need to understand: they can't afford NOT to tithe.

The bondage in which so many are held is not a new phenomenon. In 520 BC the prophet Haggai brought the following assessment to bear: *"Consider your way of life; you have sown much but reaped little, you eat but never enough to satisfy, you drink but never enough to cheer you, you are clothed but never*

[8] "Welfare Incomes Over Time," *National Council of Welfare Report*; www.ncwcnbes.net, #125, pp. 10–14.

[9] "Caring Canadians, Involved Canadians: Highlights from the 2004 Canada Survey"; www.statscan.ca, #71–542–XIE, p. 18.

[10] *The Guardian*, Friday, 24 August 2007, p. 1. "GDP" is an abbreviation for Gross Domestic Product, the total value of goods produced and services provided in a country in a given year.

warm, and he who earns wages puts them into a purse with a hole in it" (Haggai 1:5–6). "Never enough" succinctly characterizes those who mismanage their finances. The reason for the insufficiency is a function of distorted priorities. In answering why there is never enough, the prophet declares the word of the Lord of Hosts: *"My house lies in ruins, while each of you has a house you can run to. It is your fault that the heavens withhold their moisture and the earth its produce"* (Haggai 1:10). Because God's people have sought their own interests and comforts first, without regard for the will and purposes of God, heaven's blessings are withheld.

If we do not trust our heavenly Father's care and keeping, we will necessarily seek after our own interests. Our hearts will not be set on His kingdom, regardless of our rhetoric. But there will always be lack. We will not know the fullness of heaven's blessings, heaven's peace, heaven's joy, or heaven's power and authority to be about the work of the kingdom.

By way of diagnosis, some churches face a different set of problems, for theirs is a very unhealthy over-emphasis on the tithe. When it's offering time, the verse that is typically championed is Malachi 3:10: *"Bring the full tithe into the storehouse"* (NIV).

The storehouse is one of the many scriptural idioms for the Old Testament temple. The same root word is used in Nehemiah 10:37 when the newly restored people of God pledge their faithfulness: *"We will also bring the first of our coarse meal, of our contributions, of the fruit of every tree, of new wine and of olive oil to the priests at the storerooms of the temple of our God, along with a tenth of the produce of our lands."* If however, the local church is now considered the New Testament equivalent of the temple, then all of the sanctuary restrictions and prescriptions should also apply to the local church. Among many other things, that would mean that we could no longer eat pork, lobster, shrimp, crab or scallops; that roughly half of us would have to undergo circumcision, and we would have to observe the Sabbath years and the Jubilee redemptions.[11] It would also mean that we would take just as literally the other admonitions in Malachi 3, for instance the indictment against defrauding the laborers of their wages, the oppression of the widows and orphans, and depriving the aliens of justice.[12] In our day, that would have us engaging off-shore labor issues, extending committed care to the single mother and the latch-key children, and incorporating the refugee. Unlike the phrase, *"Bring the full tithe into the storehouse,"* these larger social concerns resound throughout the Scriptures, yet they are rarely highlighted or addressed when the tithe is commended.

When Malachi 3:10 is featured it either signals a literalism that is simplistic and misinformed, or betrays serious control issues on the part of senior leadership. In the worst of cases, the faithful are taught that they must bring their full tithe to the local church and only the local church. Such instruction is a legalistic, restrictive, heavy-handed and self-serving interpreta-tion of this single verse. It may well be grounded in the unredeemed fears and insecurities of the senior leader atop his pyramid. "What if my people give elsewhere? What about my vision, my plans, my budget, my mortgage?"

A healthy church lives out of a far greater, larger relational generosity. In Matthew 23:23–4 Jesus indicts the leaders of Israel and their attempts to self-justify, and He faults them at their own game, by their own legalistic rules. *"Alas for you, scribes and Pharisees, hypocrites! You pay tithes of mint and dill and cumin; but you have overlooked the weightier demands of the law – justice, mercy, and good faith. It is these you should have practiced, without neglecting the others. Blind guides!"*

The error is not that of the scribes and Pharisees alone. Jesus asks into the essence of why any of us tithe: do we give

---

[11] Leviticus 11:7, 9–10; 12:3; 25:2–4, 8–17.

[12] Malachi 3:5.

legalistically, carefully counting out the tenth, and having done that, feel self-justified? It is possible to give God His 10% and count the rest as ours to do with as we please.

The Lord's call to unbounded and unrestrictive generosity is a stark contrast:

> *"Give, and gifts will be given you. Good measure, pressed down, shaken together and running over will be poured into your lap; for whatever measure you deal out to others will be dealt to you in turn."*
>
> (Luke 6:38)

In this verse the verb "give" atypically stands without a specifying noun, begging the questions, "Give what? Give how much? How often?" But that's exactly the point: Jesus is calling forth the generosity of the kingdom of God that is so great that it cannot be legislated. When one asks, "How much am I to give beyond the tithe?" one still doesn't understand the revelation of the kingdom. How much do you want poured into your lap?

While there is only the one Malachi reference that restrictively pairs the tithe and the storehouse there are many other texts that call forth lavish, extravagant, open-handed generosity and giving far beyond the local church:

> *"I am putting your love to the test. You know the generosity of the Lord Jesus Christ: he was rich, yet for your sake he became poor, so that through his poverty you might become rich."*
>
> (2 Corinthians 8:9)

> *"If a man's gift is . . . contributing to the needs of others, let him give generously."*
>
> (Romans 12:6, 8 NIV)

> *"Sell everything you have and give to the poor, and you will have treasure in heaven; then come and follow me."*
>
> (Luke 18:22).

Believers who have a healthy understanding of kingdom finance know that God is generous and unbounded in His love. They also want to be like God. Several years ago a friend of mine, Jeff,[13] was working his way through the Book of James in his devotions. The section on practical faith made for slow reading and Jeff was challenged by the apostle's question, *"What good is it, my friends, for someone to say he has faith when his actions do nothing to show it?"* (James 2:14). At the time, Jeff was preparing to write a check to help out a family man whose business had recently bankrupted. (Though both my friend and this gentleman were members of the same church, they did not really know each other.)

As Jeff meditated on the verses he was reading, he felt that the Lord was asking him to give the man a credit card that he was to use for his food and petrol needs until he was financially re-established. Initially Jeff panicked, thinking, "Lord, you *CANNOT* be serious!" Such trust could easily be abused and he could potentially be left with some very big bills to pay.

Nevertheless, Jeff explained to the man what he'd heard the Lord ask him to do and presented the gentleman with the credit card. Jeff paid for food and petrol for eighteen months and was confident that the expenses were never compromised.

Such faithful action demonstrated the heart of God and His unbounded generosity. It also played a significant part in restoring a bankrupt life.

A stirring especially like Jeff's needs to be discerned. It could come from one of three sources. It could be demonic. But a call to generously care for a brother and his family in their need is not typically among the evil one's strategies. Nor is the restoration of a bankrupted life.

The stirrings could be motivated by natural desire. The thing is, few, if any of us, are naturally motivated to be extravagantly generous.

---

[13] His name has been changed.

If it's not demonic and it's not of our own fleshly desire, there is one further alternative. The stirring may well be from the heart of God. I would be bold to suggest that any time we feel compelled to give generously to meet another in need, we risk being *"lavishly open-handed,"* and then test the subsequent fruit.

After I had preached through the balance of this material one weekend, I had a long conversation with the host pastor about tithing. He was quite unsettled because, despite my efforts to the contrary, he felt that such a strong emphasis on the tithe would bring him and his people under the bondage of legalism. I subsequently spent several days thinking and praying through his concerns and then emailed him the following:

> "Let's compare the tithe and a quiet time. I think that it's an appropriate comparison given that generosity and prayer are essential aspects of worship, the aligning of our hearts and our heart's affections with God's. With both the tithe and a prayer time, it is essential to distinguish between the functional particulars and the motivating principles.
>
> Do I legalistically keep a prayer time? No. Is it a priority? Yes. I consider my prayer time as the first fruits of the day. I certainly try to spend some time quietly with the Lord before I turn on the computer. If I don't, the awaiting emails have the potential to hijack my prayer time.
>
> How much time do I spend? Do I legalistically 'put in the hour' when I sit down to pray? It takes me at least an hour to get settled and sorted. I usually spend far longer than an hour in prayer over the course of a day.
>
> Am I under condemnation if I spend less than an hour? *'There is now no condemnation for those who are united with Christ . . . '* (Romans 8:1). That being said, I do have the conviction that I've short-changed myself and I know that

if I continue to spend less than an hour a day in prayer, my life will soon be wonky. It will be out of balance. There will be a sense that my life has become impoverished.

Do I feel the Spirit's call every time I sit down to pray? Do I pray only when I feel His stirring? To both questions, I have to answer, 'No.' Most of the time, my quiet time begins as an established discipline. As the words 'discipline' and 'disciple' come from the same root, I understand that an undisciplined disciple is an oxymoron. As a disciple of Jesus Christ I do not pray only when I feel 'inspired.' Because my larger desire is to love the Lord with all my heart, soul and strength, spending committed time in prayer is one of the ways I nurture that love. That said, a sense of the Spirit's presence and inspiration regularly conclude my prayer times.

In many ways it's the same with the tithe. Janis and I do not legalistically give away a tenth, but it is where we start. We do not wait for the Spirit's inspiration to make this beginning. It's an established principle in our lives – we want to honor the Lord with the first fruits of our labors because we know that we are not self-made. We aren't 'inspired' to tithe, tithing is a function of discipline, and we would not be under condemnation if we were to give less than 10%. That doesn't happen because we have it settled that to do so would be to short-change ourselves. We know that if we give less than a tithe, our lives will soon be wonky, out of balance and impoverished. After we've given the tithe, we then try our best to attend as to how and where, and to what the Spirit would direct us to give."

A subsequent clarification follows. American Express card-holders are assured, "Membership has its privileges." Church has a different set of values. If we belong to a local church for the privileges it affords, something, somewhere along the line corrupted our motives. If we seek purity of heart we will gladly

embrace the spiritual reality that "membership has its responsibilities." So as not to be misunderstood, let it be clearly and
personally stated: released from a legalistic binding to Malachi
3:10, Janis and I continue to faithfully support our local church
financially with the balance of our givings. All the while, we try
to attentively obey the Spirit's stirrings to respond to the needs
of those around us. A blithe obedience that brings the full tithe
to the local church may be an abdication of the dynamic
responsibility to discern the ongoing leading of the Holy Spirit.
In Christ, there is no law but that of love.

Another signal of financial ill health in a local fellowship is a
distorted emphasis on the phrase, "sowing and reaping." In
certain circles the teaching comes off sounding like a slam-dunk
lottery. "Sow $20 into the kingdom of heaven and watch God
return $1,000 to you!"

Such teaching is crass, carnal and dishonoring to the heart
and purposes of God.

It is both materialistic and mechanistic. It is also unbiblical.

Even a casual word study on sowing and reaping makes it
clear that the phrase is most often used literally, in an
agricultural context. For example, in the Sabbath and Jubilee
years, the seventh and the fiftieth years, the land is to lie fallow.
The people of Israel are told: *"You shall not sow, nor reap"*
(Leviticus 25:11 NASB). When the prophet warns the people of
Israel of the coming judgment, one of the consequences will be
that they will, *"sow, but not reap"* (Micah 6:15).

There are then at least fourteen other distinct references to
sowing and reaping that are used metaphorically. Nine of those
explicitly deal with character. A small sample follows. *"He who
sows goodness reaps a sure reward"* (Proverbs 11:18). The opposite
is also true: *"Whoever sows injustice will reap trouble"* (Proverbs
22:8). The apostle Paul addresses both dynamics: *"Everyone
reaps what he sows. If he sows in the field of his unspiritual nature, he*

will reap from it a harvest of corruption; but if he sows in the field of the Spirit, he will reap from it a harvest of eternal life" (Galatians 6:7–8).

Further, Jesus uses the phrase metaphorically when He extends the evangelical commission to the disciples: *"One sows, another reaps. I sent you to reap a harvest for which you have not labored. Others labored and you have come in for the harvest of their labor"* (John 4:37).

Paul uses the phrase when he challenges the Corinthians about apostolic support: *"If we have sown spiritual seed among you, is it too much if we reap a material harvest from you?"* (1 Corinthians 9:11 NIV).

The remaining three references to sowing and reaping speak of the unbounded nature of kingdom blessing. As part of the Psalmist's description of divine restoration he declares, *"Those who sow in tears will reap with songs of joy"* (Psalm 126:5).

Jesus admonishes His disciples to, *"think of the ravens: they neither sow nor reap; they have no storehouses or barn; yet God feeds them. You are worth far more than the birds ... why worry?"* (Luke 12:24, 26).

(The parable that opened to the disciples the *"secret of the kingdom of God"* (Mark 4:11) begins with the words, *"A sower went out to sow."* It concludes with the promise of supernatural yield: *"some of the seed fell into good soil, where it came up and grew, and produced a crop; and the yield was thirtyfold, sixtyfold, even a hundredfold."*[14] Nowhere in the parable is there any mention of reaping, yet the thirty / sixty / hundredfold harvest is often cited as a proof-text for financial sowing and reaping. The warning about seed sown among thistles – addressed to those who, *"hear the word, but worldly cares and the false glamour of wealth and evil desires of all kinds come in and choke the word, and it proves barren"* (Mark 4:18–19) – is typically not given any consideration.)

[14] Mark 4:3–8; in Matthew 13:8 the order is reversed: a hundredfold, sixtyfold, thirtyfold.

When the apostle encourages the Corinthian church to support the believers in Jerusalem who are facing starvation he says:

> *"Remember this: Whoever sows sparingly will also reap sparingly, and whoever sows generously will also reap generously ... And God is able to make all grace abound to you, so that in all things, at all times, having all that you need, you will abound in every good work ... He who supplies seed to the sower and bread for food will also supply the seed for you to sow; he will swell the harvest of your benevolence, and you will always be rich enough to be generous."*
>
> (2 Corinthians 9:6, 8, 10)

If these commanding verses from the apostle's writings are to be determinative in our practice of kingdom finances, the subtleties of motive must be discerned, for we sow in order to meet someone else's needs – we do not "give to get."

By all means we are to sow generously: We sow righteousness, sow goodness, sow peace, and sow in the field of the Spirit. We sow generously and benevolently into ministry and missions with our hard-earned cash.

But we do so with raised expectations – with our hearts set on the kingdom of God. We do not sow to reap a bigger house, or a flashier car, or a flusher bank balance – but the fruit of the Spirit – *"love, joy, peace, patience, kindness, goodness, fidelity, gentleness, and self-control,"* a *"harvest of eternal life"* (Galatians 5:22; 6:8). We are to sow and expect to reap, *"immeasurably more than all we can ask or conceive"* (Ephesians 3:20). If we sow our old 20-inch TV, giving it to the missionaries who've returned for furlough, all the while expecting to reap a 40-inch plasma hi-def, we have impoverished expectations.

I am privileged to work very closely with a church that gives away significantly more than a tithe of their gross income. They are committed to being *"lavishly open-handed."* To be so, theirs is an ongoing commitment to rent a school facility for their meetings. They willingly embrace the aggravation of continuous set-up and tear-down of the sound equipment and seating, so that they can give extravagantly to mission, rather than be mortgage-poor and own their own building.

Several years ago it had been enthusiastically prophesied that the Lord wanted them to have their own building, that their identity within the community would be tied to a visible location. To date, that word as given has not come to pass.

However, of the 235 churches I've worked with, this church family is probably the healthiest local church of the lot. They do indeed have a very good reputation within their community, but their identity has nothing to do with their facility. It has to do with their love, their integrity, with their graced ability to accept and bless and serve.

They have faithfully sown good seed in time, talent and finances very generously, both locally and overseas. Theirs is the blessed expectation that in God's time, they will reap the abundance of kingdom harvest of healings, deliverances and salvations – the thirty, sixty, hundredfold harvest of light and life.[15]

May their tribe increase!

---

[15] See the parable of the sower, Mark 4:3–8.

5

Evangelism and Mission

"Obesity is 'contagious' study finds.

Friends help friends get fatter, a report in the *New England Journal of Medicine* indicates. Obesity can spread among a group of friends like a contagious disease, moving from one person to another in an epidemic of fat ... Having close friends who are fat can nearly triple your risk of becoming obese. The effect is so powerful that distance doesn't matter – the influence is the same whether friends live next door or 500 miles apart, according to the report in the *New England Journal of Medicine*.

The study, conducted by Dr. Nicholas A. Christakis of Harvard Medical School and James H. Fowler of UC San Diego, is the first to document the spread of obesity through a social network – a pattern of contagion most often associated with infectious diseases such as influenza and AIDS.

Instead of transmitting germs or viruses, people infected each other with their perceptions of weight. 'For example, a man attending a Thanksgiving meal may notice his brother has gained weight and conclude that it's OK to be heavier,' Christakis said.

'It's about the spread of norms from person to person,' said Christakis, a professor of medical sociology. The phenomenon worked in the other direction as well. 'People who become thinner increase the chances that their friends and relatives will lose weight too,' researchers said."[1]

This may seem a bizarre way to begin a chapter on evangelism and mission. When discerning the health of the local church in the West, however, a consideration of obesity is suggestive, for there are a number of obvious parallels.

Both excessive nutritional intake and sedentary lifestyle have been identified as the primary causes for the rapid acceleration of obesity in Western society since World War II. Some telling statistics follow: "The United States has the highest rates of obesity in the developed world. From 1980 to 2002, obesity has doubled in adults and overweight prevalence has tripled in children and adolescents. From 2003–2004, of children and adolescents aged 2 to 19 years, 17.1% were overweight ... and 32.2% of adults aged 20 years or older were obese."[2] *Statistics Canada* reports that two out of every three adults in Canada are overweight or obese.[3] Twenty percent of the population of England is obese and 37% are overweight.[4]

Spiritually, it may be that an even higher percentage of the Western Church is seriously overweight, having consumed too much, and expended too little.

A local church can only be a healthy church if it is a serving church. Church is never an end in itself, nor for itself. Dietrich Bonhoeffer, a Lutheran pastor and theologian, was an outspoken critic of both the Nazis' persecution of the Jews and the

[1] Denise Gellene, Times Staff Writer, July 26, 2007, http://www.latimes.com/news/nationworld/nation/la-sci-obesity26jul26,1,2437843.story?coll=la-headlines-nation&ctrack=1&cset=true

[2] Ogden C.L., Carroll M.D., Curtin L.R., McDowell M.A., Tabak C.J., Flegal K.M. (2006). "Prevalence of overweight and obesity in the United States, 1999–2004." *JAMA* 295 (13): 1549–55; Wikipedia, "Obesity".

[3] http://www.hc-sc.gc.ca/iyh-vsv/life-vie/obes_e.html

[4] http://www.lho.org.uk/Download/Public/8939/1/Overweight_4.gif

Lutheran Church's complicity with the Third Reich. He was incarcerated by the Gestapo in April 1943 and executed two years later. In *Letters and Papers from Prison* Bonhoeffer declared fearlessly, "The Church has fought for self-preservation as though it were an end in itself and has thereby lost its chance to speak a word of reconciliation to mankind and the world at large ... The Church is only the Church when it exists for others."[5]

A healthy church is not self-preoccupied. A church that lives and works only for itself would not be the Church of Christ. To be a church and to have a mission are not two separate things. To be itself, the Church must recognize and demonstrate that just like its Lord and Savior, it too has been sent out to the world. There is something fundamentally wrong if a local church believes that it is participating in the life of Christ through its worship and fellowship, but fails to participate actively in His mission to the world.

Two thousand years ago the early Church lived its life in marked contrast to a neighboring religious community located fifteen miles due east of Jerusalem on the northwestern shore of the Dead Sea. The Qumran community withdrew from the world, believing themselves to be "children of light," and as such, could not mix with "the children of darkness." They sought to be the pure congregation of Israel, untainted by anything impure and so segregated themselves from sinners and the unclean.

While the early Church also knew themselves to be "children of light," they understood that their call meant neither hostility to the world nor separation from the world. On the contrary, the young Church saw itself as having been sent back into the world again. Jesus did not found a monastery, but went from town to town preaching and healing, socializing with men and women across the religious and social spectrum, especially

[5] Dietrich Bonhoeffer, *Letters and Papers from Prison*, SCM Press, London, 1967, p. 211.

befriending the ritually unclean and despised. As the community of salvation the early Church understood that they could not "follow Jesus," yet retreat from the world.

The timeless call of Christ is one of dynamic tension: the faithful are to be both consecrated to the Lord and set apart from the world, but also commissioned to fulfill their redemptive mission in the world and for the world.

The local church is ever sent out to bring light into darkness, to bring salvation to all that is mashed and marred by sin, to bring life to all that is dead and dying. The joyful message of the redemption of all things cannot be kept private – it must be proclaimed and demonstrated to the world. The Church, if it is to be itself, must testify to the love of God by its love of the surrounding community, or else its preaching of good news will only be self-indulgent and empty rhetoric. Only through loving service can the Church demonstrate that this fallen world which deserted God has never been deserted by God.

The theological principles outlined above cannot be disputed by those who believe themselves to be disciples of Jesus Christ. The practice ... now "there's the rub." [6]

It is not just difficult; it is impossible to determine the absolute growth or decline of the Church in the West. Where the Gospel has never or rarely been preached, in sub-Saharan Africa or rural China for example, it is easy to demonstrate exponential growth in both individual conversions and church planting. In the West too many variables complicate any assessment. The circulation of the saints skews a census of both denominations and local churches. So too does believers' absenteeism – those who still count themselves among the faithful, but who no longer associate with an established church fellowship. With these caveats in mind, the following observations characterize the trend lines. The majority of mainline churches face a net decrease most years, while new churches, typically charismatic in theology and practice, are on the

[6] William Shakespeare, *Hamlet*, III, i.68.

increase. This numerical growth however, is mainly through transfer, not conversion.[7] One of the pastors I work with assessed his situation this way:

> "It feels rather phony to talk about our mission and evangelism activities because this is still one area in which we desperately want and need to see more fruit. We are still attracting many more of the 'dry-churched' than 'non-churched.' Most weeks now, new people are asking if they can join us, but we have yet to see a steady influx of those who don't yet know Jesus. I know that 'growth' is far more than just new converts. We are in the business of making disciples not just collecting notches on our 'conversion belt' – and we are certainly growing numerically and spiritually as a church."

If my friend's assessment can serve as a generic template for a majority of reasonably healthy churches, the following diagnostic questions require consideration. *What percentage of the local fellowship has ever personally led a non-believer to Christ?*

Has the pastor? Have the elders? Have any of the worship team or the home group leaders? How many of the committed, regular attenders have been used of the Lord to pray with someone as they gave their lives to Christ? A report of ten percent is not uncommon and the number drops to small single digits if the question is asked of those instrumental in conversions in a given year. The church research guru, George Barna, brought forth the following indictment recently:

> Let's take a look at the condition of the 77 million American adults who are churched, born-again Christians: people who have confessed their sins, asked God for forgiveness, accepted Jesus Christ as their Savior, are

[7] http://www.adherents.com/rel_USA.html

confident of their salvation ... The typical churched believer will die without leading a single person to a lifesaving knowledge of and relationship with Jesus Christ. At any given time, a majority of believers do not have a specific person in mind for whom they are praying in the hope that the person will be saved. Most churched Christians believe that since they are not gifted in evangelism, such outreach is not a significant responsibility of theirs.[8]

Very few could raise a challenge to Barna's assessment. By way of counterpoint, consider all the teaching we've received, all the books we've read, and the tapes and CDs we've listened to. If we move in charismatic circles, measure the prophecies we've received, both personally and corporately. Rehearse the ministry we've received over the years.

How different things would look if those who frequent church conferences led even one person to the Lord for every conference they've attended.

If our response is chagrined, faltering and mumbled, have we not consumed too much and expended too little?

Not all of us are anointed to be evangelists, but all of us in Christ are called to evangelism. We are not on our own, for sharing the Good News is a team ministry, *"each ... perform[ing] the task which the Lord assign[s] ... It is not the gardeners with their planting and watering who count, but God who makes it grow. Whether they plant or water, they work as a team ... We are fellow-workers in God's service"* (1 Corinthians 3:5, 7–9). Through engaging friendships, acts of loving service and faithful prayer, we are each to play a part in the conversion and sanctification of those who do not yet know of the fullness of God's love in Christ.

[8] George Barna, *Revolution*, Tyndale House, Illinois, 2005, pp. 31–32.

As such, evangelism is not so much a program as it is a way of life. We are all to be *"salt to the world"* (Matthew 5:13), not only seasoning the bland and barren lives of those who are lost and lonely, but preserving them from the rot and decay of a loveless and ultimately purposeless life. As *"light for all the world"* (Matthew 5:14) each of us in Christ ought to be living a confident authority knowing that, *"whatever is exposed to light becomes light"* (Ephesians 5:13). As Christ lives His life through us, we are to be men and women of influence.

But the goal of evangelism is not to induce the unsaved to assent to propositional truth and pray the sinner's prayer. It is to invite them to lifelong and intimate relationship with Jesus Christ. With remorse, some of us should confess that in our enthusiasm, we have misguidedly badgered and cajoled the disinterested and unengaged. Such "confrontational evangelism" is the spiritual equivalent of a drive-by shooting. As significant as conversion is, it is but one precious moment in the process of the ongoing redemption, restoration and transformation of a person's life. We are commissioned by the Risen Lord to *"make disciples"* not just converts.[9]

Metaphorically speaking, every person we meet is somewhere on God's "clock." The first twelve hours represent life before intimately knowing God's mercy and grace to us in Christ. Conversion is that moment of miracle that takes place at high noon and the second twelve hours is the time allotted as we become disciples of Jesus Christ and grow in His likeness.

This continuum of faith is reflected in the prologue to John's Gospel:

> "[Jesus] *was in the world, and though the world was made through him, the world did not recognize him. He came to that which was his own, but his own did not receive him. Yet to all*

[9] See Matthew 28:19.

who received him, to those who believed in his name, he gave the
right to become children of God . . . . "

(John 1:10–12 NIV)

A person at 4 AM on God's clock does not recognize anything
about Jesus but that His name is a swear word. Someone at
11.45 not only recognizes something about Jesus – that there is
a quality to life that is missing without Him – but with just a
little help, they are ready to receive Jesus the Life-changer and
have Him change their lives. Be it blessing for curse, forgiveness
for sin, peace for torment, acceptance for rejection, freedom for
bondage, meaning for purposelessness – receiving Jesus as
Savior marks the crossover point where one moves from death
to life, darkness to light.

To recognize and receive Jesus is but part of the process.
Thereafter, one *"believes in his name."* This is so much more
than intellectual assent, that yes, we believe that Jesus was who
He said He was, that He is the Son of God and the Savior of the
world. To believe in His name means we put ourselves under
His authority of care. He is not only Savior but Lord. And on
God's clock, we have twelve hours to respond to His Spirit's
empowering and transforming grace as we live evermore under
His authority.

All of this could be simply summarized in one sentence: Jesus
Christ gave His life *for* us, so that He could give life *to* us and
live His life *through* us.

Three stories follow. They are told by leaders of healthy
churches. The first is about forming friendships with the
un-churched and graciously helping them along on God's clock.
The second is about a prodigal's homecoming. The third marks
one very strategic way to move believers further along God's
clock.

Nev Green is the pastor of The Gathering Place, Blandford
Forum, Dorset, England. He was the one that initially asked if I
could put "Diagnostics" together to help the fellowship discern

how they were doing as a church. I asked Nev to reflect on his understanding and practice of evangelism. In part, this was his response:

"We do not believe in 'Program Evangelism' at The Gathering Place. It's too static and un-relational. What we hope to practice is 'Presence Evangelism.' Surely if there is enough of the life of Christ manifesting in our lives, those around us must be attracted to Him. Our approach, therefore, is to encourage the church family to put themselves in those places where there are people around them who will be able to 'plainly see that the Lord is with them.'

For me, that means I spend an evening in the local pub after playing squash with one of the locals, at least once a week. As a pastor it is all too easy to spend my whole life with Christians and never associate with those outside of the church. It has to be a discipline to ensure that my job doesn't encroach on these precious evenings that keep me involved in our community.

Having spent seventeen years in the Metropolitan Police Force, I feel very comfortable in the pub environment; there is nothing that the guys talk about that shocks me! At first, some people didn't believe that I am a 'vicar' (as they call me); not because of my behavior, but because they couldn't believe that a 'vicar' would want to spend an evening in the pub with the likes of them playing pool and having a pint with them. One of the guys said to me recently, 'You're the best vicar I know, because I can talk to you about anything without worrying about you passing judgment on me.'

Their acceptance has recently deepened to genuine friendship. A couple of months ago they invited me to a stag-weekend away at the Grand Prix in Barcelona. They seemed genuinely delighted that I would take a weekend off and join them. I made it clear to the guys that I looked forward to a great time, but that I would probably have to take my leave from them as the evenings progressed so as not to compromise myself. I made it clear that they were free to leave me behind and get on with whatever they wanted to do.

Before we left, one of the guys asked me if I was allowed to get drunk. I answered, 'It's not a case of whether I'm allowed to; why would I want to?' From the look on his face, that answer was obviously not one he had previously considered!

When we first arrived in Spain there was talk of some of the places that the guys wanted to hit while we were there. These were places I would certainly not be going. However, as the weekend progressed, their desire to remain together as mates outweighed any desire to do anything that I would not be part of.

Saturday night, the five of us were walking towards a pub for an after-dinner drink when I was approached by a young woman who was touting business for the local strip-club. The rest of the guys dissolved into hysterics that she picked me as her mark. I tried to explain to the woman that as a vicar, I wasn't interested in visiting her establishment. When she realized what I was trying to say, she became most apologetic. All that simply served to cause even more hilarity among the guys.

As we walked away, there was not a single moment that any of them actually considered accepting her invitation – a very different attitude from when we had arrived a few days earlier. When we returned back home, one of the guys said, 'We had such a good time all together.' The intimation seemed to be that everything that we did over the weekend was able to be done by a 'vicar' and yet, to his amazement, we had thoroughly enjoyed the whole time!

The other night at the pub, a few guys began debating whether or not the pub is haunted. They yelled down the bar and asked me if I believed in ghosts. I said 'Well, I certainly believe in the supernatural.' I then told a few 'witch doctor stories' from my experiences of ministry in Africa. One of the guys asked, 'Doesn't that freak you out?' I replied, 'Well, no, not really. The supernatural Being that I believe in is much bigger than theirs!' I went on to share some miracle healing stories I had seen firsthand.

All the while it felt as if I had earned the right to be believed. Without that earned trust, those miracle stories would have fallen on deaf ears. Instead, the pub had become very quiet. Several of the guys looked at me as if to say, 'I don't want to believe what you are saying, but I have to because I know you.' I left it there for now.

My modeling influence has had some effect on the church family. First up, everyone firmly believes that my involvement with these guys is a good work and an example that should be followed. I was actively encouraged to go on the stag weekend in Barcelona – not as vacation – but because people saw that this kind of connection to the outside world is vital for the Church. I believe that they see a hope for themselves in the fact that their pastor remains connected to the society around us. Obviously there are some who take that example and apply it to their own lives. I have seen a good number get involved in extra-church activities, doing so with the hope of carrying out one of the purposes of our existence! Of course there are, sadly, also those who agree in principle, yet still find it hard to move beyond their own set and rigidly organized lives."

The significance of Nev's anecdote must not be understated, if for one reason only. When a pastor has none of his own outreach stories to tell, his admonitions regarding outreach and mission have little by way of either authority or integrity.

The following story is told by Eddie Mason. He is the senior pastor of Southside Christian Fellowship. Eddie was introduced in the chapter on Church Atmosphere. Here he tells of meeting a couple which quickly made up lost time on God's clock.

"I go to a local country club to do my morning work out. The club has a cigar room overlooking the practice tee and the first hole, and I love going to this 'smoking room' after I've exercised. As it's always deserted in the morning, it's a wonderful place to spend time praying and meditating in the presence of the Lord. One morning the assistant manager of the club took me aside and said, 'Rumor has it that you are a preacher. Is this true?' Not knowing what was coming next, I simply responded, 'Yes.' She then asked, 'What are *you* doing in the smoking room?' When I told her that I was spending time with the Lord, she got extremely excited and said, '*That's* why you're glowing!'

The next time I was at the club, she pulled me aside and began to tell me about her fears for her children. We spoke for a while, I shared some Scripture with her and told her I would pray for her and her family. A few days later she emailed me and told me that she and her husband were having some trouble. She confided that she was making plans to leave him and move to Florida. Towards the end of the email she asked if I would consider meeting to counsel them.

The three of us sat in my office and began to talk about what was going wrong. They had met at Bible school, but under the stress of working and raising a family they had drifted away from the Lord and each other. As we talked, the husband began to tell me about the prayer encounters he used to have with the Lord. He talked of times when he would just weep or laugh, times that were so rich he did not want the prayer time to end. The wife also spoke about her experience of the sweet presence of the Lord.

A week later I asked the woman how things were going with her husband. She told me it was like they were on their honeymoon. They wanted to be with each other again. Their hunger for God had returned and they were both spending time with the Lord.

She did end up moving to Florida, but it was with her husband and children. I still stay in touch. They are excited about their future and their whole value system has changed. They are quick to say that as the joy of the Lord has filled their home, the things that previously seemed so important have lost their appeal. Now they want nothing more than to be in the center of God's will."

Dr. Dave Mullen is the senior pastor of Church of the Living God in Manchester, Connecticut. Dave first invited me to preach at the church in April of 1997. Many subsequent visits have made Church of the Living God feel like a home away from home. I asked Dave to reflect on their commitment to mission and what it has meant both for the church and those involved in outreach.

"When asked about the missions emphasis at Church of the Living God, I have to stop and think about what it is that we do here. Missions have become such an integral part of who we are, it's just something we do as part of the natural expression of our life as a church. It hasn't always been this way. In 1994 we received a significant move of God's Spirit in our midst. This visitation continued for ten years and the impact continues to reverberate and shape who we are and what we do today. Prior to 1994 we gave to missions. Since then we both give and go.

One of the things God has placed a special emphasis on

in our collective heart is the Great Commission – particularly the little word 'go' (Matthew 28:19). Through relationships with missionaries we were already connected to, we began to explore the feasibility of sending out our own teams on short-term trips. These trips are normally two weeks in length and involve both work and ministry. In the past ten years we have seen well over six hundred people (including numbers of repeats) travel to and minister in Latin America, Asia, Africa, Europe and the Caribbean. About one-half of our church family, including our youth, has been on at least one mission trip. Eighty percent of our youth have been to a foreign field. My own children have been on every continent except Antarctica!

We work at maintaining a high profile for missions and outreach. The entire congregation will lay hands on a departing team and commission them on 'Send-off Sundays.' We generally send off three or four teams per year. I will use each of these occasions to encourage people to get their passport and be open to the voice of the Holy Sprit with the expectation that he will say, 'Go.' Each time a team visits a new nation, we hang the national flag of that country in our sanctuary. It then becomes a visual reminder of our commitment to go and do our part to extend the kingdom and make a difference.

We spend several months training our teams and this builds great team camaraderie. And following the trip, the energy an entire team brings back into the church is much more significant. This has all contributed to an infectious missionary spirit.

In order to ease people into a foreign short-term missions experience we provide a number of local opportunities for service. These include work in local soup kitchens, volunteering at the local homeless shelter, inner-city work with the homeless in New York and, recently, relief work in the wake of hurricane Katrina.

Some of our foreign trips are a bit 'edgier' than others and it is rare that someone will go on one of these trips without some previous local experience in serving and ministering to others.

One result of our missions commitment to both give and go is that we have developed a global vision and passion. I often marvel at what a little New England church can accomplish by way of kingdom impact. We also enjoy a sense of being connected to the global Church. We feel plugged into what Jesus is doing around the world and that gives us a larger field of vision than simply our own locale and issues. We now have several full-time missionaries on the field as a result of their short-term experience. We have found that 'going' will ruin a person for the normal and mundane.

The personal impact of a missions trip on the individuals who go varies widely. Very few people come home the same. At the very least there is the realization (often accompanied by a bit of guilt) of the vast difference in our level of affluence and comfort compared to so many of the nations of the world. Almost all who go, return with a much higher commitment to the giving of their finances. Our missions giving is significant and any specific appeal for a missionary or outreach project is responded to with generosity. One of our men has made it his life goal to get to the place where he and his family live on twenty percent of his salary, allowing them to give the other eighty percent to missions.

The most common result we see in people returning from a missions trip is a notable willingness to say, 'yes.' People become much more willing servants of Christ when they see the difference they can make by giving of themselves. Numbers of our young people have made educational and career direction changes. Instead of simply becoming lawyers they are studying international law. Studies in economics are aimed toward helping third-world countries. Language majors are looking to work with the U.N. or in foreign consulates. Giving is great, but going makes a great personal difference.

The downside to this commitment to going and not just giving? Other than missing the good people who have left the church for the mission field, I can't think of any."

On God's clock, no one hour is more important than another. Because His mercy is unconditional, there is not a single hour when God loves us any more, or any less than He does right now. The Lord loves the guys kibitzing in Barcelona as much as He loves those who serve the poor on a short-term missions trip. Jesus described the loving heart of God this way: *"Your heavenly Father . . . causes the sun to rise on good and bad alike, and sends the rain on the innocent and the wicked."* He then challenged those who were listening: *"If you love only those who love you, what reward can you expect? . . . There must be no limit to your goodness, as your heavenly Father's goodness knows no bounds"* (Matthew 5:45–48).

There is not a single person we meet that doesn't need to know more of the kindness, the mercy, the compassion and the goodness of God. A further revelation of that love always heals, and saves, and redeems . . . something. On God's clock, more than anything else, it's love that moves us along.

A friendship that is driven by an agenda other than love is always compromised. "Friendship evangelism," while it may sound healthier than "program evangelism," can easily be compromised. If we befriend the un-churched in order to lead them to Christ, the friendship may suffer outcome corruption. Regardless of our motive, we've entered into the relationship with an end in view. We may then love with less than unconditional care if we don't get the response we seek.

Most of my un-churched friends would be unwilling to be

my friend if they felt that I was out to convert them. Yet most of them have said something like, "You're not like the other born-againers that I know. You're different. I know I can talk to you and know that you'll listen. And when you have something to say, I know it will be something I want to listen to."

This chapter began with the provocative line, "Friends help friends get fatter." In the context of God's clock, the line could be rewritten: "Loving friends help friends get loved." The healthiest churches help their friends get loved.

In Acts 14:8–9 Paul *"fixed his eyes"* on the crippled man from Lystra. The verb in Greek comes from the root *atenidzo*, meaning "to stretch, to strain, to attend." The words "tension" and "attentive" are derived from this root. Other translations express the meaning of the word in different ways: Paul *"observ*[ed] *him intently"* (NKJV); *"looked directly at him"* (NIV); *"fixed his gaze upon him"* (NASB). However it's translated, *atenidzo* is something more than general looking about. To simply "see" in Greek is the word *eidon*. Miracles like the healing of the lame man in Lystra only occur when we pay loving attention to those around us. Jesus said, *"Look, I tell you, look around at the fields: they are already white, ripe for harvesting . . . "* (John 4:35).

Many of us need to confess that most of the time, we *"have eyes but fail to see"* (Mark 8:18 NIV). Indifference, self-preoccupation and inattentiveness keep us blind to the grace that the Spirit is working in those around us and purposing to call forth through us.

Just as in the physical, a sedentary lifestyle shortens our spiritual life expectancy.

Conclusion

I wrote the balance of this book through an unseasonably hot and calm summer. While working on this chapter, I took a long-anticipated break one afternoon. A forty mile an hour wind was blowing. I packed up my windsurfing gear and headed for the beach. It was deserted.

For most people it was a nasty afternoon weather-wise. Wind blown sand stung my face and arms as I rigged my sail. The spray that was ripped from the breaking waves left a damp mist on anything that could stay put in the gale. But for a wind-starved sailor, these days are few and far between. I was so eager to get out on the water I forgot the mast base that connects my sail to the board and had to run back to the lakeside parking lot to retrieve it.

In Hebrew and Greek, the words *ruach* and *pneuma* have a double meaning and are used for both "wind" and "Spirit." As an illustration, high-performance windsurfing has compelling parallels to life in the Spirit.

When the wind is howling, it is not a sense of duty that compels me to lash my board to the roof of the car, nor is it onerous to rig my sail. Desire and delight are what motivate me. I don't "have to" go sailing, I "get to."

For my type, strong winds are a gift. Regardless of our impassioned incantations, windsurfers cannot make it be windy.

When it does blow, however, my prior commitment is tested. I need to maintain a measure of physical fitness in order to have the strength and stamina required to sail big winds. My gear needs to be in good repair. I have to be able to avail myself of an opportune wind. (Here the illustration breaks down a bit. Availability has, by times, caused a measure of familial conflict!)

Once I'm on the water, high-wind sailing requires continuous attentiveness to the constant fluctuations in the subtleties of the ever-changing wind velocity and direction.

When conditions are scary-fast, any loss of concentration and focus result in a spectacular crash. When blasting over the waves at forty miles an hour, hitting the surface of the water is like smacking concrete. Mercy abounds, however, for though I've had the wind knocked out of me many times, I've yet to sustain a serious injury. There are serious consequences to my inattentiveness though, for my gear has not been so fortunate. Over the years I have broken a mast, bent several booms, sheared the stainless steel hook on my harness, delaminated one board and fallen through several sails. The wages of windsurfing sin is at least death to the rigging.

Seventeen years ago, several church friends bought me custom license plates for my birthday. They read, RIG BIG. Those two words are short for the rather cheeky expression, "Rig big or don't rig at all." Though the statement is a little arrogant, rigging the largest sail possible sounds the call to be powered by as much of the wind as one can manage, and then some!

Rigging big holds discretion, humility and courage all in dynamic tension. If I'm over zealous and launch with too big a sail, I'll be overpowered and will be forced to spill the wind from the sail or get slammed. Fearfully rigging too small a sail, I'll not only be underpowered, but very frustrated knowing that there's so much more I could be harnessing.

The dynamics involved with rigging big can all be applied to both a vital life in the Spirit and the corporate health of the local church. If we are open and responsive to the work of the Spirit in our midst, our lives will be marked by desire and delight, gratitude, commitment, strength, stamina, availability, attentiveness, discretion, humility and courage.

We too will know that it is always a travesty to let good "wind" go to waste.

It is a rather unexpected transition to shift from the exhilarations of high-speed windsurfing to the mundanities of an annual physical exam, but such is the stuff of life. Suppose Joe Blog goes for his check-up. The doctor takes his vitals, shines his little light in his eyes and ears, has him breathe deeply and cough. He then proceeds to tell Joe that he needs to lose thirty pounds, get regular exercise and reduce his cholesterol levels. Joe leaves the doctor's office and is basically on his own. It is up to him to improve his health. There's a good chance that little in Joe's life will change, unless there's some sort of crisis. A heart attack is a great motivator.

Now that your reading of *Vital Signs* is nearly complete, you've had your spiritual check-up. Both your personal and corporate spiritual health has been assessed. No one of us gets an absolutely clean bill of health. For each of us, there are at least a few things that need to change. On one hand, it's just the same as attending to one's physical health. It's up to each of us to improve our spiritual health and vitality.

It's up to us to learn the disciplines that make us more of a worshiper. Someone else's consecration doesn't bring our hearts into alignment with God's.

It's up to us to deepen our relationships, to invite someone out for coffee, or in for a meal. We ought not to wait to be the ones invited out.

It's up to us to bring a greater vulnerability, integrity and accountability to bear in our primary relationships. No one else can work purity of heart into us.

It's up to us to choose to be generous. Come offering time, do you want to pass your wallet to the person sitting next to you and ask them to give what they hear the Spirit is saying you should give?

It's up to us to be praying for those in our spheres of influence and attending to the fullness of life the Spirit of God is yet calling forth in those around us.

Further, lest things be misconstrued, our spiritual wellbeing is not like a drop-down menu select. We cannot be considered spiritually healthy if we are a passionate worshiper but a stingy giver. We can't pick a single aspect of *Vital Signs* and run with it alone. Not if we want to know the fullness that is ours in Christ Jesus.

That's on one hand. On the other hand, we ought not to see Dr. Jesus just once a year for our annual check-up. We ought not to drag ourselves to Dr. Jesus only when we feel unwell. In 1 Corinthians 1:30 Paul writes, *"By God's act you are in Christ Jesus; God has made him our wisdom, and in him we have our righteousness, our holiness, our liberation."* Jesus is our life, our health, our vitality. The more we abide in Him, the healthier, happier and holier we will be personally and corporately. It is His life, in us, that is our health.

On profession of faith, we are justified in Christ. Our sin has been forgiven and we have peace with God (Romans 5:1). Justification is a completed work. Thereafter, we are being sanctified as the Spirit *"comes to the aid of our weakness"* (Romans 8:26). The word "sanctify" comes from the Latin root, *sanctus*, meaning "holy." Through the ongoing work of the Spirit, we are being made whole and holy, and that means we are all in process. The health and holiness of the Church is also in process.

On January 3rd, 1521, the German reformer Martin Luther was excommunicated for his scholarly objections to current church practices. He had presented to the church authorities his "Ninety-Five Theses" which assessed the ill health of the institutional church Luther served. One sample of his critique follows. In Thesis 86 Luther boldly asked: "Why does not the pope, whose wealth today is greater than the wealth of the richest [German], build the basilica of St. Peter with his own money rather than with the money of poor believers?"

Though Luther's critiques were solidly grounded in responsible Scriptural exposition, those who received his assessments were both unrepentant and openly antagonistic. Luther wrote a rebuttal titled, "An Argument in Defense of All the Articles of Dr. Martin Luther Wrongly Condemned in the Roman Bull." In the course of his refutations he cited Matthew 13:33, the parable of the leaven which a woman mixes into three measures of meal until it is leavened through and through. Luther commented,

> The new leaven is the faith and grace of the Spirit, Who does not leaven the whole lump through at once, but gently and slowly makes us altogether like Himself...
>
> This life is not therefore righteous, but growth in righteousness, not health but healing, not rest but exercise. We are not yet what we shall be, but we are growing toward it. This process is not yet finished, but it is going on. This is not the end but it is the road. All does not yet gleam in glory, but all is being purified.[1]

In this regard, what is true of the individual is also true of the local church. Every local church is not what it shall be, but it is growing toward it. This recognition of process has significant consequence in terms of commitment to a local fellowship. Over fourteen hundred years ago, Benedict of Nursia wrote a little treatise that defined the life of a monastic community. *The Rule of St. Benedict* subsequently became determinative for centuries of monastic life and practice. The five vows of poverty, chastity, obedience, the conversion of manners and stability delineated monastic calling and vocation. The fourth and fifth vows may be unfamiliar to many readers. The conversion of manners signals the ongoing commitment to the transformation and

[1] *Works of Martin Luther*, Philadelphia: Muhlenberg Press, 1930, p. 14.

sanctification of personal character. As to stability, Benedict wrote his *Rule* in part to address the problems created by the wandering monk. Given both the limitations of the individual and the limitations of a given community, the vow of stability means that the monk renounces the vain hope of trying to find the perfect monastery. It doesn't exist. The Trappist monk Thomas Merton insightfully commented: "[The vow of stability] implies a deep act of faith: it is the recognition that it does not much matter where we are or whom we live with, provided we can devote ourselves to prayer ... All monasteries are more or less ordinary."[2] A monk is to stay put in a particular monastery because that was where the Lord had placed him and by the grace of God, he is to play his part in making it a better monastery.

Just as there are no perfect monasteries or convents, so there are no perfect churches either. The church will be *"radiant ... without stain or wrinkle"* (Ephesians 5:27 NIV) only when presented to Christ as His perfected bride. Until then there's some work to be done and that requires of us a ruthless honesty, for *"If we claim to be sinless, we are self-deceived and the truth is not in us"* (1 John 1:8).

Given the current circulation of the saints, church health would improve markedly if we each took a vow of stability, stayed where the Lord had placed us and dedicated ourselves to try to bring more of the grace of God to bear greater fruit within that particular fellowship. If instead, we are continuously on the move, it's rather like disregarding a doctor's prognosis in the hopes of finding someone who will tell us that everything is just fine. Our health depends on dealing with what ails us. And corporately, we have the choice – we either make our church better or worse. What needs to be discerned is what isn't as it should be.

[2]   Thomas Merton, *The Sign of Jonas*, Image Books, New York, 1953, p. 19.

It's one thing for a doctor to tell someone that they have six months to get their cholesterol levels down. It's far more sobering to hear that drastic action is required, that a cancer has to be cut out. A person may be so unsettled by the news that they don't even hear the doctor say that after the surgery, he expects them to make a full recovery.

There are times when the doctor sits someone down and tells them the bad news. Further tests were required; those results are in. A systemic toxicity has been discovered and the talk is no longer about "if" but "when." They're told to get their affairs in order.

There are a similar range of scenarios when church health is assessed, for all churches are somewhere along a continuum of health. If after a diagnosis some arbitrary numbers are assigned, there are a few churches that are eighty percent healthy. If you're part of such a church, give thanks, every day! And understand that membership in such a fellowship is both a privilege and a challenge. Like an elite track and field athlete, expect the bar to be continuously raised. It is a signal of the robust health of the church. With the challenge comes the response. As one host said to the gathered congregation, "Given what's been laid before us, we need to up our game."

Dynamic spiritual health implies continuous pursuit of and response to the supernatural. I recently preached at a conference in Maidstone, Kent. The weekend's theme title was "Touching Heaven, Changing Earth." That phrase concisely renders the ministry mandate that must ever define church health and vitality. Among many other things, it means commitment to continuous change. Kingdom priorities mean that life and ministry cannot ever be static. Things cannot ever stay the same. Not if we expect the Spirit to work in our midst, *"immeasurably more than all we can ask or conceive"* (Ephesians 3:20). A posture of confident expectation and anticipation needs to outweigh the anxiety of not knowing what is before us.

A committed diligence is also required, for there are forces that seek to work against the growth of the Church. Entropy is one of the least sinister, but most pervasive of the lot. It can be defined as the gradual decline into disorder. For example, the majority of us have put ourselves on a diet or an exercise program, and done so with the greatest of intentions. We've done marvelously ... for three days. Entropy sets in and our resolve is eaten away more quickly than the pounds we hoped to shed.

Without discipline and diligence, spiritual entropy reduces us to the same old, same old, often as quickly as our resolve to diet or exercise is lost. A deep and rich spiritual life, while a gift, does not happen arbitrarily. Devotion, humility, gratitude, generosity and loving service do not grow to maturity without sacrifice. Without resolve, the sins of pride, complacency, indifference, compromise and self-concern grow like weeds in an untended garden.

Five hundred years ago the fathers of the Reformation – Wycliffe, Hus, Luther, Calvin, Zwingli, Bucer, Melancthon – addressed the systemic toxicity of the Church of their day. As was noted above, they brought their study of the Word of God to bear on the false doctrines, malpractices and corruption of leadership that had created a very sick Church.

Roughly one hundred years after the initial reformation, the familiar cycle of renewal and decline was already in force. After a period of vitality and restoration, spiritual entropy had set in, and laxity, indifference and complacency had once again taken their toll. A Dutch theologian, Johannes Hoornbeeck, diagnosed the evident degeneration he saw in the Church of his day. As a learned man he used a Latin phrase to prescribe the cure: *Ecclesia reformata semper reformanda,* "The reformed church, always in need of being reformed." His working thesis was simple: spiritual reformation is never a complete work.

Attentiveness, not dogged determination, is required. The verb tense in Hoornbeeck's phrase is known as the passive obligatory. It means that the reforming work that we, as the Church, continuously need comes not from within, but is always a work of the Spirit upon us. The transformation we need is not self-motivated. The Church is the recipient, not the agent of its own change. The health of the Church is always a work of grace, lovingly applied over time.

This work of continuous reformation is voiced throughout the apostle Paul's writings:

> *"Though our outward humanity is in decay, yet day by day we are inwardly renewed."*
>
> (2 Corinthians 4:16)

> *"Conform no longer to the pattern of this present world, but be transformed by the renewal of your minds."*
>
> (Romans 12:2)

> *"You must be renewed in mind and spirit, and put on the new nature created in God's likeness."*
>
> (Ephesians 4:23–24)

> *"Put on the new nature which is constantly being renewed in the image of its Creator and brought to know God."*
>
> (Colossians 3:10)

Both personally and corporately, anything less than ongoing renewal and reformation means that we have surrendered to forces of entropy that will be our demise.

Further down the continuum of health, there are churches that are sixty percent healthy. Each and every member of such a church has a choice. Their individual decisions make their community of faith healthier or sicker. As there is no church in which the Spirit of God is not purposing renewal and restoration, there is hope. In spite of the problems, the resistance to change, and ungodly mindsets and attitudes; in spite of the pastor, or the leadership, or the power brokers of the institution, one can make a difference. By the power of the Spirit, kingdom leaven has a mysterious influence that over time transforms the entire lump.

But what is to be done if, once assessed, the conclusion is irrefutable: the church is only twenty-five percent healthy? The question is a really challenging one, for somewhere towards the end of the continuum of health there are some churches that are unsustainable. If the lump has become rancid, no amount of leaven and no amount of time can transform it.

Fourteen years ago I labored for two years attempting to re-mandate a twice-failed church plant. We were heading for a "three-peat." As I was tremendously discouraged, a friend kindly invited me to the St. Louis church planting conference hosted by his Vineyard church. During the four days together one of the Vineyard's regional overseers handed out copies of the official "Church Plant Autopsy Report." Produced in 1986, it contained the prioritized results of interviews with twenty-two pastors of failed Vineyard church plants.[3] That report objectified what we knew intuitively. Our core group was functionally unwilling to embrace a missional model of church and engage in outreach.

A number of factors brought us to a moment of crisis. With very real grief, we began asking, "Lord, are You releasing us from this church and this denomination?" A month later we were praying, "Would You?"

When the trend lines are so obviously on the downhill slide and you've worked heart and soul to make a difference, yet the majority of your church family have not and evidently do not want to answer the Spirit's call unto kingdom fruitfulness, the rhetorical question raised by the prophet Isaiah resounds: *"When a farmer plows for planting, does he plow continually?"* (Isaiah 28:24 NIV). There comes a moment when it's time to move on.

---

[3] The report was subsequently reproduced in the book, *The Quest for the Radical Middle: A History of the Vineyard*, Bill Jackson, Vineyard International Publishing, Cape Town, South Africa, 1999, p. 140.

On, because in Christ we never quit. The cynic can easily review the sorry history of the Church, weigh it in the balance, and find it wanting. The shameful persecution of the Jews, the crusades, the trials of heretics and the burning of witches; ecclesiastical colonialism, wars of religion; the silence, complicity and indifference to slavery, racism, sexism and war; the identification with unjust and unrighteous systems of society, government and thought; the neglect of the poor and indifference to the marginalized are more than enough to evidence a sickness unto death.

So too does graceless and unstudied preaching, boring and often antiquated forms of worship, externalized religiosity, spiritless traditions, irrelevant and powerless ministry, domineering leadership, morality divorced from the complexities of life, judgmentalism and intolerance, legalism and the self-aggrandizement of ecclesiastical functionaries at all levels – reason enough for those who continue to believe in "God," but who will have nothing to do with the Church.[4]

None of these travesties should be justified or excused. Nevertheless, in the face of all human failures, corruptions and compromises, the Church of Jesus Christ has prevailed for two thousand years. It has done so because of one reason alone. From the dawn of human history God's renewing and restoring grace continues to prove stronger than any human failing.

The preaching of Christ crucified continually creates faith and the Spirit of Jesus is constantly guiding and sanctifying and bringing continuous renewal. The redemptive history of the Church is vindication of Jesus' promise:

> *"The Spirit of truth . . . dwells with you, and will be in you . . .*
> *[He] will teach you everything and remind you of all that I have*
> *told you . . . He will guide you into all the truth . . . He will take*
> *what is mine and make it known to you."*
>
> (John 14:17, 26; 16:13–14)

4 Cf. Hans Kung, *The Church*, Image books, New York, 1976, p. 49.

Similarly, the apostle Paul concludes his first letter to the church at Thessalonica with a wonderfully comprehensive prayer:

> *"May God himself, the God of peace, make you holy through and through, and keep you sound in spirit, soul, and body, free of any fault . . ."*
>
> (1 Thessalonians 5:23)

Our spiritual health and holiness is that which God Himself purposes. Our spiritual health and holiness is that which Jesus Christ has appropriated for us. Our spiritual health and holiness is that to which His Spirit is ever calling, ever stirring, ever imparting grace.

We would do well to regularly take a deep breath and say, "Thank You, Jesus."

Such habitual gratitude would keep us in good company. In terms of sheer numbers, the most frequent type of prayer the apostle Paul prays is that of thanksgiving.

> *"I am always thanking God for you. I thank him for his grace given to you in Christ Jesus; I thank him for all that has come to you in Christ."*
>
> (1 Corinthians 1:4).

> *"I thank my God every time I think of you . . ."*
>
> (Philippians 1:3)

> *"In all our prayers to God, the Father of our Lord Jesus Christ, we thank him for you . . ."*
>
> (Colossians 1:3).[5]

After thanksgiving, what Paul prays for most often, and what he asks after most explicitly, are prayers for more wisdom and

[5] Paul wasn't particularly happy with the Galatians' conduct. It is the single letter he writes that does not contain a declaration of the apostle's gratitude.

knowledge. This fact more than underscores his candid admission that, *"we do not know how we ought to pray"* (Romans 8:26).

Because the apostle knows there is so much more to be appropriated, he prays,

> *"that the faith you hold in common with us may deepen your understanding of all the blessings which belong to us as we are brought closer to Christ."*
>
> (Philemon 6)

> *"I pray that the God of our Lord Jesus Christ, the Father of glory, may give you spiritual wisdom and revelation in your growing knowledge of him."*
>
> (Ephesians 1:17 NET)

> *"We ask God that you may receive from him full insight into his will, all wisdom and spiritual understanding, so that your manner of life may be worthy of the Lord and entirely pleasing to him."*
>
> (Colossians 1:9)[6]

These are prayers the Lord loves to answer, as the apostle James assures us:

> *"If any of you lacks wisdom, he should ask God and it will be given him, for God is a generous giver."*
>
> (James 1:5)

Before we pray boldly, we should anticipate what could be called "the cycle of grace."

God freely gives further revelation to those who seek Him, and so something more of the heart and the nature and the purposes of God are continuously made known. The reception of the gift necessarily means that we can't keep living as we did prior to the revelation.

---

6 See also Ephesians 1:18–19; 3:17–19; Philippians 1:9–11.

*"God is light, and in Him there is no darkness at all. If we claim
to be sharing in his life while we go on living in darkness, our
words and our lives are a lie. But if we live in the light as he
himself is in the light, then we share a common life, and the
blood of Jesus his Son cleanses us from all sin."*

(1 John 1:5–7)

A number of terms are used to describe this dynamic of grace –
refining, pruning, cleansing, purging. In one way or another,
radical revision must necessarily follow revelation if we are to
live the truth we've received.

It's one thing to come before the Lord to receive His
blessing. It's quite another to submit to the transformation He
purposes in order to make us like Christ. This we need to know
when we sing songs that ask for the fire of God to fall. Even
heaven's fire requires fuel.

We're it. Any further revelation and release of spiritual
blessing consumes the remaining impurities and dross of self.
The unsettling events of 2 Samuel 6 tell out this truth in the
extreme. King David had recaptured the Ark of God that
the Philistines had stolen. He mounted the Ark on a wagon
and, at one point, the oxen pulling the cart stumbled and it
looked as if the Ark might fall off.

A man named Uzzah tried to help. Presumably with the best
of intentions, he attempted to steady the Ark, yet was, *"struck
down for his imprudent action"* (2 Samuel 6:7). His death reads
rather severely, until one understands the blatant disregard that
preceded the judgment. David knew better than to put the Ark
on an ox cart. Months after Uzzah's death, David retrieved the
Ark from the house of Obed-Edom, but this time employed,
"bearers of the Ark of the LORD" (2 Samuel 6:13), thereby
complying with the explicit instruction given to Moses as found
in Numbers 4:5–15. When it's time to move, specially consecrated poles were to be slipped through the rings on the side of
the Ark and the Kohathites, *"the guardians of holy things"*

(2 Samuel 3:28; 4:15) were to do the lifting. All of this because, *"they must not touch the sacred things, on pain of death."*

The name Uzzah is one of the Hebrew words for "strength." It is used in Psalm 132:8, *"Arise, O LORD . . . you and the ark of your might* [uzzah]*"* (NIV). It is used in Psalm 46:1, *"God is our refuge and strength* [uzzah]*, an ever-present help in trouble"* (NIV). When the story of the Ark's capture and Uzzah's death is retold in 1 Chronicles 15, and it's all done and sorted, King David led in a hymn of praise in which he admonished the people of God to, *"look to the LORD and his strength* [uzzah]*; seek his face always"* (1 Chronicles 16:11 NIV).

We can never fulfill the Lord's purposes in human strength and initiative. Uzzah's untimely death tells of at least three graphic life-lessons. The presence of God cannot be corrupted or compromised. The presence of God and human presumption cannot coexist for very long. And no one can "touch heaven" whilst being willfully disobedient and expect to get away with it.

Such is the work of refining fire. If we understand the cycle of grace, this ought not to cause dread. I have the following quote taped to my study wall:

> The option of absolute despair is turned into perfect hope by pure and humble prayer. One faces the worst, and discovers in it the hope of the best. From the abyss there comes, unaccountably, the mysterious gift of the Spirit sent by God to make all things new, to transform the created and redeemed world, and to re-establish all things in Christ.[7]

This is the third phase in the cycle of grace – a greater abiding and a fuller communion with Christ. Through the perpetual drawing by the One who loves us more than we love ourselves, the Lord fulfills in us His own High Priestly prayer:

[7] Thomas Merton, *Contemplative Prayer*, Image Books, New York, p. 25.

> *"May they all be one; as you, Father, are in me, and I in you, so also may they be in us."*
>
> (John 17:21).

All of this can be simply summarized: *if* revelation, *then* refining. Any attempts to skip straight to abiding short-circuit the process.

It is up to each of us to discern how it is the Spirit is directing us, or correcting us, or redirecting us. If we are to become healthier, happier and holier, we need to hear what He is saying to *us* as the Church. And we must be able to discern His voice from all the other voices that clamor for our attention. One distinction we must be able to make is between conviction and condemnation. The Revealer convicts; the accuser, one of the names of the evil one, condemns.

When we have fallen short of God's purposes, either willfully or in ignorance, the Spirit's conviction brings the opportunity for repentance and restoration. For instance, the Spirit sent Nathan to bring King David's adultery to light.[8] As the prophet told a story about another man's overt sin, David, a *"man after God's heart,"* became indignant. Nathan went for the jugular: *"Thou art the man!"* (2 Samuel 12:7 KJV).

David had a choice. He could either take the prophet's head off or he could humble himself and repent. The King said to Nathan, *"I have sinned against the LORD"* (2 Samuel 12:13).

Some pastors and others in leadership may need to stand before their church family and say something like, "I've just finished reading a book that has left me gutted. I need to apologize to you; I ask for your forgiveness and I ask for your prayers. Though I've tried my best, there are a number of things that I've got seriously wrong. By the grace of God I hope to make things right . . ."

---

[8]   See 2 Samuel 12:1–6.

Some church members need to make similar confession to their pastors and leaders.

None of us are as we yet shall be. The Church, when healthiest, never forgets that there is more grace to be imparted and appropriated. With the first century believers, we would do well to pray continuously,

> *Remember, O Lord, your Church,*
> *Save it from every evil*
> *And perfect it in your love.*
> *Gather it together from the four winds*
> *And lead it sanctified*
> *Into your kingdom you have prepared for it.*
> *Yours is the power and glory forever.*[9]

---

[9] *The Teaching of the Twelve Apostles*, 10.5, *Ante-Nicene Fathers*, vol. 7, Hendrickson Pub., Peabody, Mass., 1994, p. 380.

We hope you enjoyed reading this New Wine book.
For details of other New Wine books
and a range of 2,000 titles from other
Word and Spirit publishers visit our website:
www.newwineministries.co.uk